HEINEMANN
PLAYS

JANE LIDDIARD

Moving On

Three Play Scripts for the Classroom

Activities linked to the National Curriculum by
Jane Liddiard

Heinemann

Heinemann Educational Publishers
Halley Court, Jordan Hill, Oxford OX2 8EJ
A division of Reed Educational and Professional Publishing Ltd

OXFORD MELBOURNE AUCKLAND
JOHANNESBURG BLANTYRE GABORONE
IBADAN PORTSMOUTH NH (USA) CHICAGO

First published 1999

03 02 01 00 99
10 9 8 7 6 5 4 3 2 1

ISBN 0 435 23325 4

Original design by Jeffrey White Creative Associates; adapted by Jim Turner
Typeset by ☚ Tek-Art, Croydon, Surrey
Cover illustration by Rob Hefferan
Cover design by Philip Parkhouse Design Consultancy
Printed and bound in the United Kingdom by Clays Ltd, St Ives plc

CONTENTS

Notes to Teachers   v

Football Crazy   1

Hoping for Charlie   65

The Russian Bracelet   133

Speaking and Listening Activities

   Football Crazy   168

   Hoping for Charlie   171

   The Russian Bracelet   174

Help Notes   177

ACKNOWLEDGEMENTS

My grateful thanks go to the following.

Fred Stockton, Head of English, Woodcote High School, for his advice and help with *Football Crazy*, and his permission to use material for the Help Notes.

My friend Pat Barden for her medical advice for *Hoping For Charlie*; my friend and former colleague Anne Lee, English teacher, and Year Nine pupils at Wilson's School for their help and advice with *Hoping for Charlie*.

My friend and former colleague Sue Christofides, English teacher, and Victoria Eyers, Michelle Greaves and Gemma Shakespeare, pupils at Wallington High School For Girls, for their help and advice.

And finally my sons, Alastair and James, for their invaluable help and comments.

NOTES TO TEACHERS

About the Play Scripts

These plays have been written for Year Eight upwards and cover strong but topical themes such as girls wanting to break into traditional boys' sports, serious illness, bullying by girls, and theft. Each play is set in a different school – mixed comprehensive, co-ed boarding school and girls' grammar – to include a much wider range of educational experience. The staging of each play is also different so that there is a variety and range of dramatic form. There is a clear need for contemporary drama in schools that is relevant to pupils' daily lives, which they will find realistic and interesting, and which raises issues that are challenging such as illness, looks, friendship, gender roles and bullying. The plays examine questions of conflict, courage, loyalty, morality, prejudice, the law, the joys and pains of friendship, irrational dislike, triumph and disaster. Above all, they are intended to show that humane regard for our fellow human beings is fundamental to a peaceful and caring society – but it isn't always that easy.

The National Curriculum

Each play, and the activities for Speaking and Listening and Writing that follow, are based on the requirements of the National Curriculum. The activities take into account a wide range of tasks and abilities providing the teacher with a comprehensive system of assessing Key Stages 3 and 4. When working on the Oral Activities pupils should take notes of their own work and work presented to them by others in the class so that these can be used for the Writing Activities.

Help Notes

There are additional notes for *Hoping for Charlie* (see pages 66–67), and Help Notes appear at the back of the book as a guide for the activities; these are designed to be useful for both pupils and teachers, and to enable pupils to progress at their own pace and level.

About the Author

Jane Liddiard taught English for 23 years, including GCSE and A-level, has been widely involved in acting and producing drama both in schools and with adults, and is now a playwright. She wrote the first two plays in a set of four play scripts for Year Sevens, *Stepping Up*, published by Heinemann for schools.

Football Crazy

List of Characters

Pupils

Charmian	Brian
Debbie	Wesley
Karen	Grant
Rina	Georgina
Emma	Pushpa
Gary	Kelly
Martin	Conroy
Lloyd	Ali

Teachers
Miss Anderson, PE (Miss A)
Mr Williams, PE

Others
Mrs King, Charmian's mother
Mr King, Charmian's father
Charlene, Charmian's sister
Terry Thomson, United Girls' Football Team Manager (Manager)
Kingsley Boys' Junior Football Team, players 1–10 (KB Player 1–10)
United Girls' Football Team (G Players 1–10)
Borough Park Girls' Football Team
Kingsley Boys' Fans (KB Fans)
Girl Fans
United Fans
Borough Fans (Boro' Fans)
Journalists 1–6
Photographer(s) (Pho'grapher)
Referee
Woman Police Constable (WPC)

FOOTBALL CRAZY

Scene One

Characters: Charmian, Rina, Emma, Karen, Debbie, Miss Anderson.

The girls' changing room after a Games lesson. The girls enter noisily. Charmian throws her track suit top down.

Charmian	I hate netball! It's so boring.
Karen	It's all right. At least it's not dangerous like hockey.
Charmian	I want to play football.
Debbie	*What!*
Charmian	Football. You know, that game where you chase a ball about and kick it into goal.
Debbie	That's a boy's game.
Charmian	Don't be daft. Anybody can play these days. You just have to have the skill.
Karen	Do you think there'd be enough girls for a team in our year?
Charmian	It doesn't have to be in our year. We could have under 14s.
Debbie	Huh, the boys'll love that!
Emma	Yes, can you see Scott Parker lining up with the girls?
Charmian	He doesn't have to line up with us. We won't play with them. We'll have our own teams.
Emma	Oh, come off it, Char, old Williams won't have a girls' team.
Charmian	Well, I'm going to see Miss Anderson about it at break.

Emma   Bet she's not for it.

Charmian   She might be.

Emma   Well, Mr Williams'll never let you.

Charmian   He's got to. He can't stop us playing.

Debbie   You're mad.

Charmian   Just wait and see.

She marches off.

Emma   Bet Miss Anderson soon tells her where to go.

Karen   No, don't think so. She's pretty good about things like that but Mr Williams won't have it. He wouldn't want anything interfering with his precious boys' team.

Rina   He's not allowed to discriminate.

Emma   Who cares? Who wants to get muddy knees and bruises? She's welcome to it.

Debbie   You can talk. You can't even play netball properly.

Emma   So what? At least Char's right about that. It is a stupid game.

Miss Anderson, the PE teacher, enters. The girls get up quickly and try to look busy.

Miss A   Come along, you girls. The bell is about to go. You'll be late for your next lesson. Haven't you lot started changing yet! What's been going on?

Debbie   Don't know, Miss.

Miss A   I do. Too much talking. Now get a move on!

Debbie   Yes, Miss.

Miss Anderson goes. Debbie makes a face behind her back. The others laugh.

Scene Two

Characters: Charmian, Miss Anderson.
Charmian is talking to Miss Anderson in the
Sports Office.

Miss A   So what's this all about, Charmian?

Charmian   I want to play football, Miss.

Miss A   I know that, but what do you want me to do about it?

Charmian   I want you to ask Mr Williams if he'll set up a girls'
football team, Miss. I mean, I really want to play and
I want to be in a team. I'm good enough, I know I am.
You've got to believe me. I just need the chance.

Miss A   Yes, OK, Charmian, slow down a minute. We could
have a problem here. It might not be possible to set
up a girls' team.

Charmian   Why not?

Miss A   Well . . . it's a question of timetables and facilities
and –

Charmian   But I played football in my junior school.

Miss A   I know.

Charmian   And I was in the school team.

Miss A   Yes, but it's different here.

Charmian   How come?

Miss A   Well . . .

Charmian   Mr Williams doesn't want girls to play, does he? It's
not really about the timetable and all that. It's about
me being a girl, isn't it?

Miss A   No, it's true about timetabling and staff. The
teachers are always complaining about it.

Charmian   I played in my last school and there weren't
any problems.

Miss A Yes, but it's different here. At your last school you were quite young and boys and girls could play in the same team, but you're in your teens now and you're growing up and you would have to have a completely separate team.

Charmian Yeah, so?

Miss A So I don't think we'll be able to have a girls' team. There aren't enough PE staff.

Charmian (*getting up angrily*) That's just an excuse! I knew all the teachers would be against me!

Miss A Charmian, sit down for a minute. You can't go storming about like this. You just get people's backs up that way.

Charmian (*sitting down again*) Look, Miss, you've got to help me. All I want is to play football.

Miss A I appreciate that, Charmian, but it's not that easy and it's not going to make me very popular with Mr Williams and the other PE teachers and, quite honestly at the end of the day, I don't think it will be possible but I will look into it – although I can't promise you anything. OK?

Charmian Oh, thanks, Miss. You're really great!

Charmian runs off. Miss Anderson shakes her head and sighs.

Scene Three

Characters: Miss Anderson, Mr Williams.

Mr Williams enters in a track suit carrying some footballs in his arms. Miss Anderson calls after him. He is startled and drops the balls. They scrabble about retrieving them.

Miss A	Sorry.
Mr Williams	Don't think anything of it. I've only spent half an hour collecting them up.
Miss A	Mervyn, I must speak to you. I think we've got a problem.
Mr Williams	Not Greene again.
Miss A	No, for once it's not him. It's Charmian King.
Mr Williams	Ms Strange's class?
Miss A	Yes –
Mr Williams	Her brother Carl's in the Senior Football Team, one of my best players.
Miss A	Yes, and –
Mr Williams	Very good he is too.
Miss A	Mervyn, will you let me get a word in edgeways? Charmian wants us to set up a girls' football team.
Mr Williams	*A what?*
Miss A	An all-girls team.
Mr Williams	No chance. We haven't got the facilities, or the time.
	He starts to walk away.
Mr Williams	I can barely find enough time for the boys' team.
Miss A	Wait, Mervyn. You can't dismiss it just like that.
Mr Williams	Why not?
Miss A	Because . . . because you can't.
Mr Williams	Listen, Linda, she can't play and that's that. It's got nothing to do with me personally. It's the facilities and the timetable and the staff. All of which we have not got. Besides, the boys would never wear it. A girls' team? I'd have a riot on my hands.
Miss A	They may have to if she makes a fuss.
Mr Williams	No. She'll have forgotten all about it in a week's time.
Miss A	I don't think so.

Mr Williams Well, let's wait and see, shall we?

He walks off as Miss Anderson tries to continue speaking to him.

Scene Four

Characters: Debbie, Karen, Rina, Gary, Charmian.

It's lunch break. Debbie, Karen and Rina are standing around talking. Gary enters dribbling a football. He weaves in and out of the girls.

Gary And Gary Greene picks up a really difficult pass making it look so easy, goes round one defender, two, three, and shoots. Goal!!!

Gary kicks the ball offstage.

Debbie Get off, Gary.

Karen Get lost.

Gary Don't you like my brilliant play?

Debbie What's brilliant about it?

Gary You don't appreciate nothing, you don't.

Debbie Not you anyway.

Gary I'm going to play for England one day.

Debbie Oh, yeah?

Gary Oh, yeah.

Karen Is that going to be before or after you've joined the best team in the world?

Gary You can laugh. Just you wait and see. (*to someone offstage*) Oi, you, give me my ball back.

The ball is thrown to him. He does a series of fancy exercises with it. Charmian enters talking to herself.

Charmian	Stupid. Stupid.
Rina	Are you all right, Charmian?
Charmian	No. Miss had a talk with Mr Williams but he won't let us have a girls' football team.
Gary	Football? You want to play football? Don't be daft. Girls are no good at football.
Charmian	Who says?
Gary	Come on, then.

Gary starts to dribble the ball. Charmian chases after him, tackles and gets the ball. Then she lets it fly offstage.

Charmian	Goal!
Gary	Ah, beginner's luck. I wasn't ready.
Debbie	(*making fun of him*) Oh, come on, Gary. She beat you.
Karen	Beaten by a girl, Gary.
Rina	Easy peasy.
Gary	Yeah, well, it's different on the pitch.
Charmian	I played in my junior school. I was top goal scorer.
Gary	It's different at this school. We're not a bunch of little kids. We're lads. Here, what you done with my football?
Charmian	(*pointing offstage*) Over there.
Gary	Get it then.
Charmian	Get it yourself.

He goes off grumbling. The girls laugh again, but Charmian still looks upset.

Debbie	Don't take any notice of Gary. He's just mad because you beat him.
Rina	He's all right, don't worry.
Charmian	It's not him.
Karen	Do you really want to play football? In school and all that?

Charmian	It's the only thing I've ever wanted to do. I mean, I dream of playing for England one day.
Karen	With the *men*?
Charmian	No, they wouldn't have that but there'll be an England women's team one day, you'll see. They've got one in cricket.
Karen	I suppose there's a first time for everything.
Rina	You might be another Gary.
Charmian	Over my dead body!
Rina	Or his!

Scene Five

Characters: The Kingsley Boys' Junior Football Team, a crowd of Kingsley Boys' Fans, Charmian.

The football team enter dressed in their full Kingsley High kit of green and white.

KB Players	(*chanting*) We are the champions. We are the champions.
	They do a series of exercises then stand up and clap their hands above their heads.
KB Players	We are the champions.
	They do another set of exercises and throw and pass the ball to one another. Then they clap their hands above their heads, and turn and point in the same direction downstage.
KB Players	Oi!
	A spot comes up on Charmian dressed in her light blue football kit. She stands holding a football and looking at the boys. The team laugh at her. She

turns away. The team go off. A crowd of football supporters enter noisily. They are sporting the Kingsley High colours. They jostle about, wave scarves and rattles. Then they wave their scarves above their heads.

KB Fans   Kingsley. Kingsley. Kingsley for the Cup. We are the champions.

They act as though watching a football match and then as though a goal has been scored.

KB Fans   Yess!! One-nil, one-nil, one-nil, one-nil.

They clap and do a Mexican wave.

KB Fans   Goal! Two-nil, two-nil, two-nil, two-nil.

They shout and point towards Charmian.

KB Fans   Oi!

They laugh. Lights fade on supporters. Charmian turns to the audience.

Charmian   I will play. They can laugh, but I will play.

Scene Six

Characters: Charmian, Mr King, Mrs King, Charlene, Journalist, Photographer.

All the family, except Charmian's brother Carlton, are in their lounge. Charmian enters.

Charmian   You wanted to see me?

Mr King   Yes, girl, me and your mother want to chat with you about this business at school.

Charlene   Yeah, it's really getting on my nerves. She never stops talking about it. She's making a right idiot of herself. Football, I ask you!

Charmian	You shut up, you're always keeping on at me. It's got nothing to do with you.
Charlene	You've got to be joking. I'm a laughing stock at school.
Charmian	Well, why don't you get lost then? I don't want your opinion anyway!
Mrs King	Now, don't start, you two. We're supposed to be having a family discussion in a civilised manner. I don't want no arguing.
Charmian	Tell *her* that then.
Charlene	Speak for yourself.
Charmian	And where's our Carl if we're all meant to be here?
Mrs King	He's got football practice. You know there's a match on Saturday.
Charmian	Bet you wouldn't have let me go if it was him we were talking about.
Mrs King	Now you know that's not true.
Charmian	Huh!
Charlene	You can't play anyway, you're a girl.
Charmian	Shut up, you.
Mr King	Come on now, this bickering is getting us nowhere.
Charmian	What are we going to talk about anyway?
Charlene	You making a right fool of yourself.
Mr King	Enough. Now, girl, your mother and me are really concerned. We hear you've been making a fuss at school and all that, and now the newspapers want to see you. What's going on?
Charmian	Dad, you know I want to play football. You know that's all I've ever wanted to do but they won't let me.
Charlene	I'm not surprised. Why can't you do something normal like athletics?
Charmian	What like you, you mean? You've got to be joking.

Charlene	At least I'm not causing a load of trouble at school.
Charmian	Pull the other one. Anyway, it's nothing to do with you!
Mrs King	Come on, girls, we've got to get this sorted out. If we're not behind Charmian, how's she going to manage?
Charlene	Who cares? It's a waste of time. The school isn't going to let her play and that's that. She should just pack it in.
Charmian	No!
Mr King	That's not very, helpful, Charlene. Your mother and me have always supported you and your brother in your sports. Why shouldn't your little sister get the same?
Charlene	Because it's a waste of time, that's why, and because she's on to a loser.
Mr King	Now be sensible. Is it fair that she should be prevented from doing what sports she wants to just because it's inconvenient?
Charlene	No, I suppose not but they're not going to let her though, are they?
Mr King	So we should give up now?
Charlene	Yeah, what's the point?
Mr King	The point is that if you don't fight for your rights you'll never get anything in life.
Charlene	So what?
Mrs King	Look, all your father is saying is that we've got to decide whether we're going to back your sister or not. I say we stick together.
Charlene	And have the papers and everything involved?
Charmian	You have to because they'll help us.
Charlene	Make a fool of you, more like.
Mr King	No, I don't think so. I think they'll be on Charmian's side but the school isn't and what we've got to

	realise is that we've got a fight on our hands but if we all agree to back Charmian then we do it as a family, together, (*looking directly at Charlene*) nobody going behind her back and criticising her and making fun of her. Is that clear?
Charlene	(*grudgingly*) Yeah, all right.
Mr King	Good. Right then, the first thing this means is that your mother and me will have to be around while this is going on to make sure it doesn't get out of hand, and to talk to the school or whatever.
Charmian	But I thought Mum was going to Grenada soon?
Mrs King	I was, darling, but I can't go away while all this is going on.
Charmian	But Mum –
Mrs King	Now don't you worry about nothing. Your father and me have discussed this and I can go another time. This'll all blow over soon, you wait and see. The important thing is that we're here to support you.
	The doorbell rings. Mr and Mrs King go out.
Charlene	(*whispering*) Typical! Mum's had to give up her holiday all because of you.
Charmian	I didn't ask her to.
Charlene	No, but she's going to, isn't she?
Charmian	Back off, ratface!
	The Kings return with a journalist and photographer from the local paper.
Mr King	This is someone from the local *Advertiser* who wants to interview Charmian. I said we wouldn't mind.
Journalist	Thank you. (*to Charlene*) Can we get some pictures first and then I'll speak to you after?
Charlene	It's not me you want. It's her (*pointing at Charmian*). I'm the normal one.
Journalist	Oh.

Mr King	Charlene!
Charlene	Just a joke.
Pho'grapher	Right, I'll get some piccies of the little lady first and then we'll have a happy family fun photo.

The photographer clicks away.

Pho'grapher Right. That's it. Good. Great. Marvellous.

Charlene groans but Charmian is pleased to be photographed and she poses quite happily as the photographer snaps away.

Charlene (*slipping offstage unseen*) He's not taking any photos of me. Nerd!

Journalist OK, that's enough pictures of the little lady, I think. Now how about one of you and your lovely sister?

The journalist looks around for Charlene.

Journalist Oh, she seems to have gone.

Charmian Trust her!

Scene Seven

Characters: Charmian, Karen, Debbie, Rina, Emma, Martin, Lloyd, Gary, Brian, Wesley, Grant.

Some weeks later. Karen, Debbie, Rina, Emma, Martin and Lloyd are talking. Lloyd has his arm round Emma and Martin is sitting with Rina. Debbie is reading a magazine.

Martin Anyone going out tonight? Debbie wants to go to that new disco place that's just opened up.

Rina What, *Tramps?*

Emma Yeah, that's it. Everybody's going. You get a free soft drink and there's a really brilliant DJ.

Karen   (*sarcastically*) Oh, wow. Can't wait.

Rina   I don't think my mum and dad'll let me.

Lloyd   They won't know. Tell them you're round at Karen's.

Emma   Yeah, come on it's going to be really great.

Lloyd   Carlton might be there for Debbie!

Debbie   (*looking up*) What?

Emma   (*laughing*) We said if you come with us to the disco we'll arrange for Carlton to be there waiting for you with his tight trousers on.

Debbie   Shut up, you two. It's not funny.

Lloyd   It is. I'm cracking up. Carlton King!

Debbie   Look, I'm going if you're going to be stupid.

Lloyd   Sorry. So are you coming with us?

Debbie   Dunno.

Martin   Karen?

Karen   I've got a lot of homework tonight.

Martin   What? You've got to be joking. Who does any homework?

Emma   She does. She's a right boff.

Martin   Don't you fancy that boy in Year Ten, Mr Tate's class. We'll ask him to take you. What's his name?

Debbie   Damian.

Emma   (*mocking her*) Damian. Ooh, Damian!

Debbie   Yeah, it's almost as stupid as Lloyd.

Emma   Watch it, Carrington.

Debbie   Watch it yourself.

Lloyd   Well, we're going, aren't we, babe?

Emma   Yeah.

Rina   (*holding her waistline*) Do you think I'm getting fat?

Karen   *You*? No chance.

Rina	I think I'll go on a diet.
Karen	You'll disappear.
Rina	And I've got spots.
Lloyd	You're all right. You girls, you're always worried about your weight, or your hair, or your make-up, or your clothes, or –
Rina	All right, don't go on about it.
Martin	Charmian King isn't. She wants to be one of the boys.
Karen	No, she doesn't. She just wants to play football.
Lloyd	It's a boys' game.
Karen	That's rubbish! Anyone can play. Why shouldn't girls play if they want to?
Lloyd	Because they'll be useless at it. They can't tackle, they can't shoot properly and they'll be stopping every five minutes to check their make-up and comb their hair.
Karen	I can't believe you're saying this.
Lloyd	And she's making a right idiot of herself in the papers and everything.
Emma	Yeah, I wouldn't stick my neck out for that.
Debbie	You wouldn't stick your neck out for anything except all that make-up.
	Charmian enters and looks around suspiciously. She knows they've been talking about her.
Emma	(*all nice*) Hi, Char, how you doing?
Charmian	What's it to you?
Emma	Only asking, that's all.
Charmian	So what've you been saying about me then?
Rina	We were only talking about you trying to have a girls' football team.
Charmian	So?
Emma	Don't you mind everybody knowing?

Charmian	No.
Emma	Yeah, but with everybody looking at you and that?
Charmian	I don't care, let them look. I'm not giving up now. Luckily, Mum and Dad are a hundred per cent behind me.
Karen	You're all very sporty in your family, aren't you?
Charmian	Suppose so.
Karen	I mean, Charlene's brilliant at something.
Charmian	Yes, she does athletics for the school and the county.
Debbie	And Carl's really great at football.
Emma	Oh, get you.
Rina	Debbie goes to watch him in all the school matches.
Debbie	So?
Rina	Nothing. Just saying, that's all.
Debbie	Well, don't. It's none of your business.
Rina	I didn't mean anything. Don't get so stressed.
Charmian	Charlene's coach reckons she might be good enough for the national team soon.
Karen	That's brilliant.
Emma	Will she be famous?
Charmian	Probably. Especially if she gets medals and things.
Emma	I want to be famous. I want to be a model.
Debbie	You've got to be really beautiful to be a model.
Emma	Not necessarily. You've just got to look good in photographs.
Karen	Photogenic, you mean.
Emma	Yeah, whatever. Anyway, you couldn't do it. You've got glasses.
Karen	What's wrong with that?
Emma	Nothing, except it doesn't make you look very nice. I mean, I don't know any models who wear glasses.

Karen	That's because they can wear contact lenses.
Emma	Well, you're not pretty enough anyway.
Debbie	What makes you think you're so marvellous yourself, Emma?
Emma	Everyone says so.
Rina	Modelling's good, though. It's something either boys or girls can do.
Debbie	Yes, but hardly anybody makes it to the top. (*to Emma*) I doubt if you'll get anywhere near it with that figure.
Emma	Come on, Lloyd, let's go. The company in here stinks.
Lloyd	You coming, Mart?
Martin	Yeah.
	Emma, Lloyd and Martin leave.
Karen	Good riddance.
Debbie	Here, look at this.
	They all crowd round the magazine. Gary enters unseen by the girls.
Rina	I think that model's really ugly.
Debbie	Emma'll be all right then.
Karen	Uh, don't fancy him.
Rina	No, he's all right. He's got nice eyes.
Karen	Rubbish haircut, though. Look at it.
Debbie	Yeah, but look at the rest of him.
Charmian	Modelling's like athletics. No one's going to stop you wanting to do it because you're a girl and Charlene's always on at me about my football. She was threatening to tell Mum that I wear my kit to school under my school uniform.
Gary	You what?
Rina	Gary! What are you doing here?
Debbie	Nosing in on other people's conversations, as usual.

Charmian	You'd better not tell anyone, Greene, or I'll get you.
Gary	All right, all right, keep your hair on. Don't worry, your secret is safe with me.
Charmian	It had better be.
Rina	What are you doing here, anyway?
Gary	(*holding up the local newspaper*) Have you seen this? Charmian's all over it. Her picture and everything. Look.

He spreads out the newspaper and they all look. Karen reads.

Karen	*School Slammed In Football Tiff. Former junior school football champion, Charmian King, has slammed her school for refusing to run a girls' football team.*
Rina	Does your mum know about this?
Charmian	Yes.
Debbie	Ssh.
Karen	*Charmian, who played for her junior school team and could clearly run rings round the boys and score a few goals, is determined to see this through. 'I'm not going to be beaten. Once they see I can play they'll want me in a team,' she told our reporter.*
Gary	No chance.
Debbie	Shut up, Gary.
Charmian	Mum's asked to see the Head. She's cancelled a trip to Grenada for this. She was going out to see her family.
Gary	Wish my mum would go off to Grenada – and never come back.
Rina	Gary!
Gary	Didn't mean it. Well, only a little bit.
Debbie	You're famous now, Char.
Gary	Infamous, more like.

Brian, Wesley and Grant appear. They jeer at Charmian.

Brian   Ya, football crazy.

Wesley   Think you can play. You're mad.

Grant   Bet you couldn't score a goal if it was a mile wide.

Gary   Get lost, O'Neill, or I'll re-arrange your face.

Grant   Try it, Greene.

Wesley   Bet he wants to play in the girls' team.

Gary   It's better than yours, anyway.

Grant   I'm not in a team.

Gary   That's what I mean. Snap's more your game.

Brian   We'll get you for that.

Gary   What, and tickle me to death with the Joker?

Brian   Better watch it, Greene, I won't forget what you said.

Gary   Oh, hard man.

Wesley   You're getting above yourself.

Gary   Well, I need to grow a bit.

Grant   You're mad, King. Think you can play as well as the boys? Never.

Brian, Wesley and Grant go.

Rina   Don't mind them, Charmian.

Charmian   I try not to but I hate it when everyone's whispering and laughing at me.

Gary   Don't worry, I'll look after you.

Karen   (*laughing*) In that case, I'd be worried, Char!

Rina   Come on, don't bother about them. They're only jealous.

Karen   Keep with us. They won't keep on at you if you're with us.

Charmian   Thanks.

They go.

Scene Eight

Characters: Mr Williams, Miss Anderson.

Mr Williams enters the staffroom and angrily throws a newspaper down on the coffee table in front of Miss Anderson.

Mr Williams   Have you seen this, Linda?

Miss A   No. What's wrong?

Mr Williams   That King girl. All over the local paper claiming discrimination and heavens knows what.

Miss A   Well, it's true, Mervyn.

Mr Williams   I know it is but there's nothing I can do about it. We can't change everything at the drop of a hat for one girl.

Miss A   Perhaps we should change it for all of them then.

Mr Williams   Thanks for your support.

He picks up the paper and reads.

Mr Williams   Here, what's this? I did not say girls are no good at football. I said it's no good girls wanting to play at the moment. The school timetable's already set for the year. They didn't even mention that. Why do they have to twist everything you say? Makes me look a right fool.

Miss A   No comment.

Mr Williams   What?

Miss A   Only joking.

Mr Williams   It's not funny, Linda.

Miss A   No, the Head's not going to like it either. Bad publicity for the school.

Mr Williams   I can't help it. She should think of these things and do something before it gets out of hand.

Miss A	I don't think she could have foreseen this one, Mervyn.
Mr Williams	No? Well, I know who's going to carry the can for it – and it won't be the Head, I can tell you.

The telephone rings. Miss Anderson answers.

| **Miss A** | Staffroom . . . Yes . . . OK, I'll tell him. |

She puts the phone down.

| **Miss A** | Guess what? That was the Head and she wants to see you in her office straight away. |
| **Mr Williams** | Here we go. As if I hadn't got enough on my plate already! |

He throws the paper down and storms out.

Scene Nine

Characters: Mr Williams, Journalists 1–6, Photographers, The Kingsley Boys' Junior Football Team (Players 1–10), Girl Players 1–10, Charmian, Gary.

Journalists and photographers are massed in a group waiting for Mr Williams. He enters and mayhem erupts. Flashbulbs and questions are fired at him. He tries to escape but they surround him, shouting and jostling.

Mr Williams	(*holding up his hands*) One at a time or I won't answer anybody!
Journalist 1	Would you like to comment on the Charmian King affair, Mr Williams?
Mr Williams	No.
Journalist 2	How do you feel about girls playing football?

Mr Williams   No comment.

Journalist 3 Is it true that you won't allow a girls' team in your school because they might show up the boys?

Mr Williams   That's rubbish. It's just not practical, that's all.

Journalist 3 Isn't that just an excuse, Sir?

Mr Williams   No, it isn't!

Journalist 4 She's entitled to be treated the same as the boys, though, isn't she? Do you think the family will sue?

Mr Williams   How should I know?

Journalist 5 Charmian King reckons she could get compensation.

Mr Williams   That's nonsense. We don't have to provide any particular sporting activity at the school. Besides, if she's that good she should have no problems getting into a local girls' team, should she? Look, I've got enough on my plate without this.

Journalist 5 Can I quote you on that?

Mr Williams   You can quote me on anything you like as long as it's accurate.

Journalist 6 Could you tell us whether it's your school's policy to exclude girls from traditional boys' sports?

Mr Williams   No.

Journalist 5 'No' it isn't school policy, or 'No' you can't tell us?

Mr Williams   Just no.

Journalist 6 Is it true that you personally are opposed to girls playing football, Sir?

Mr Williams   Don't be ridiculous.

Journalist 3 But you won't have a girls' team, though, will you, Sir?

Mr Williams   Will you get off my back!

Journalist 2 Are you going to fight this to the bitter end, Sir?

Mr Williams   Leave me alone.

Journalist 1 Are you liable to be sacked because of this, Mr Williams?

Mr Williams   GO AWAY!!

*He waves his arms at them shouting angrily. The
journalists and photographers scatter. Mr Williams
stands alone on stage. He puts his head in his
hands and groans.*

Mr Williams   This is a nightmare.

*The lights dim. Mr Williams collects a blanket and
pillow and lies down pulling the blanket over his
head. He moans and turns over. Charmian leaps
dramatically on stage in an aggressive pose. She is
dressed in full football kit, wearing a mask and
carrying a pitchfork. She circles round Mr Williams
and then prods him with the pitchfork. He yells out.
Charmian laughs and dances triumphantly offstage.
The Kingsley Boys' Junior Football Team, minus
Gary, enter. They jeer at Mr Williams, pulling faces
and pointing.*

KB Player 1   Missed.

KB Player 2   Again.

KB Player 3   Missed.

KB Player 4   Again.

KB Player 5   Oh, no, another goal against us.

KB Player 6   Not another one!

KB Player 7   What? Another one, another one?

KB Player 8   Yes.

KB Player 9   Two-nil?

KB Player 10   Yes.

KB Player 1   Oh, no.

KB Player 2   A load of girls' blouses!

*They stand in girlish poses and say, 'Ooh!' A
whistle blows.*

KB Player 1   Lost 22-nil.

KB Player 4   It's Mr Williams' fault. He's spending too much time
on the girls' team.

Mr Williams No! No!

The team make faces at Mr Williams and jeer at him. Then they trip off with very light feminine steps. A girls' team enter, led by Charmian.

G Player 1 Great shot, Char!

G Player 2 Again.

G Player 3 Right on target.

G Player 4 Again.

G Player 5 Oh, yes! Another goal for us.

G Player 6 Another one!

G Player 7 What? Another one, another one?

G Player 8 Yes.

G Player 9 22-nil?

G Player 10 Yes.

Charmian Oh, great!

G Player 2 Better than the boys any day!

They stand in triumphant poses. A whistle blows.

G Player 1 Won 22-nil.

G Player 4 It's Mr Williams. He's a cool manager.

Mr Williams No! No!

Mr Williams moans and turns over. Gary enters out of the spotlight in the dark.

Gary (*in the dark*) Please, Sir, I want to be a ballet dancer.

A spot immediately comes up on Gary. He is wearing a tutu, tights, ballet shoes and a hair band, and stands in a ballet pose.

Mr Williams (*screaming*) No, no! You're my best junior player!

Spot fades.

Mr Williams No, please, don't tell me my best player wants to be a ballet dancer! No-o!!

Mr Williams throws off his blanket and sits up.

Mr Williams *THIS IS A NIGHTMARE!!*

Scene Ten

Characters: Rina, Debbie, Karen, Emma, Gary.
The girls are chatting.

Rina   Did you see Charmian on telly last night?

Debbie   Yes, she was great. She's famous now.

Emma   You don't get famous by being on the telly for five seconds.

Debbie   Jealous.

Emma   No, I'm not. She must be mad wanting to play football. I don't.

Rina   What's the matter? Worried you'll get your nails chipped?

Gary walks up to them. He is still wearing his ballet costume. The girls burst out laughing.

Debbie   Gary, what are you doing?

Emma   You'll get arrested walking around like that.

Rina   Or beaten up.

Karen   Come on, tell us. What you doing?

Gary   I'm in a sketch for the School Revue, only I got a bit hungry so I'm going to get a Mars and a Coke from the machine.

Karen   We've just told you, you can't walk around like that.

Gary   Nah, I'll be all right.

Emma   I think it's an improvement.

Gary   Oh, very funny. Did you see Charmian on the telly?

Karen   Yes, we were just talking about it.

Debbie   Emma's jealous.

Emma   Shut up, Debbie.

Rina   What did you think?

Gary	Fantastic. Brilliant. Great.
Emma	What? Are you in love with her or something?
Gary	What if I am?
Debbie	It'll break Rina's heart, that's why.
Rina	Shut up, Debbie.
Gary	Is that right, Rina?
Rina	I just like you, that's all – as a friend.
Emma	Oh, yes.
Rina	Mind your own business, Emma.
Emma	Mind yours!
Gary	Cor! The girls are arguing over me.
Debbie	Don't kid yourself, Gary.
Gary	They can't help it. It's my wonderful good looks.
	The girls laugh at this and every other comment he makes.
Debbie	Back of a bus, you mean.
Gary	My irresistible charm.
Karen	Your stupidity, you mean.
Gary	My perfect body.
Emma	Your short, fat, hairy little body, you mean.
Gary	Here, what's this? Thought you lot were meant to be my friends?
Debbie	We are but we don't want you getting too big-headed.
Karen	Weren't you meeting Charmian yesterday for a practice in the park?
Rina	Yes, how did you get on?
Gary	Talk about great, she was fantastic. Better than Scott Parker any day. He'd better watch out.

Scene Eleven

Characters: The Kingsley Boys' Junior Football Team, Charmian, Gary, Miss Anderson.

The team, minus Gary, run on. They have a warm-up session practising throw-ins and so on. Charmian walks on in her kit, carrying a football. They immediately stop and look at her, then sing to the tune of 'You'll Never Walk Alone'.

Team   Charmian King, Charmian King, are you really so daft
As to want to play football like us?
Walk off our school pitch,
Walk away to your home,
Walk on all alone
'Cos you'll never play like us.
You'll never play like us!
Walk away, walk away, walk on all alone
'Cos you'll never play like us.

The boys clap their hands above their heads and then one of them snatches the ball from Charmian. They pass it around as she tries to get it back then it's thrown behind them. They link arms forming a wall with their hands in front of them as though she's taking a free kick. Every time Charmian tries to get past they block her. Finally, she gives up and moves away. They cheer and run off. She moves down stage.

Charmian   Everybody's on at me just 'cos I want to play
football and I've made a fuss about it. Is it worth it?
Dad says he doesn't mind but I know he hates the
publicity. Mum's had to cancel her trip to Grenada
to see her family, just for me. My brother Carl's
disgusted because I'm drawing attention to myself
in school and he's getting a lot of stick from his

mates, and my sister Charlene won't even speak to me she thinks I'm so daft. And even if they do let me play in a team I bet it will be just a few people having a laugh.

She sits down feeling very sorry for herself.
Gary enters.

Gary   Char? Char, are you OK?

He sits down beside her and puts an arm around her shoulder.

Gary   It's all right, Char. Don't let it get to you. They'll have to let you play eventually.

Charmian   Oh, yes? Why?

Gary   Because the school doesn't like all the bad publicity, that's why. I heard old Williams talking to Miss Anderson and he said the Head'd given him a right rollicking and now he's got to support our girls joining the local FA Football League and let you practise here if you want to.

Charmian   Really?

Gary   Straight up. God's truth and all that.

Charmian   I didn't know we had a League.

Gary   Yeah, it's just getting off the ground. There's one or two regular teams but there's a whole lot of new ones starting up. You can have a team from anywhere in the county and, get this, United supports one of the teams.

Charmian   *United?*

Gary   Yes, but of course the girls won't play at their Kingsley Park ground. That's only for the professionals but one of their coaches is going to coach and be manager of the girls' team. I think it's at the Sports Centre that they play. And, listen to this, they're looking for new talent. You should go for it.

Charmian   Really? Do you think I'd get in?

Gary	Dead easy. You'll knock spots off everybody.
Charmian	Oh, fancy playing for *United!*
Gary	Here, don't get too carried away. It's only the girls' team. I mean, it's not the real team. I mean, even I couldn't get into that. Well, not yet, anyway. So now you can show them, Char. Easy.
Charmian	It's all right for you, Gary. You don't have to fight and show yourself up. It's really horrible when everyone gets on to me, pointing and having a go at me just 'cos I want to play football.
Gary	They have a go at me too 'cos I'm supporting you and I go round with Rina and them, but I don't listen. That's what you've got to do. You've got to show them, right?
Charmian	But how?
Gary	By beating them at their own game, that's how. I mean, who scored most goals for the school last season? Gary Greene, that's who. Who scored the winning goal in the County Schools' Championship? Gary Greene, that's who. And whose hat-trick got us the Milkshake Trophy? Gary Greene's, that's who.
Charmian	Yeah, well, I'm not even in a team yet so there's no point in telling me about scoring goals.
Gary	You will be, sooner or later and that's a promise. Then they'll see.
Charmian	Do you really think so?
Gary	I know so.
Charmian	(*giving him a hug*) Ooh, Gary!
Gary	Here, hold on. Somebody might see.
Charmian	You're really great, Gary.
Gary	Yes, I know.
	Miss Anderson enters.
Miss A	You two look cosy. What are you cooking up? (*they both spring apart*) I'd like to speak to you, Charmian –

Charmian	We weren't doing anything, Miss . . .
Miss A	– about this football business. On your own preferably.
Charmian	Gary.
Gary	What?
Charmian	Gary!
Gary	Oh. Oh, yeah. Right. Just going. Ta-ta, Char. Bye, Miss.

Gary pretends to go but hangs around out of sight, listening.

Miss A	Now, Charmian, a very important meeting's been held. The Head, the Deputy Heads, Heads of Year. You name it, they were there and your name was on the agenda.
Charmian	About me playing football?
Miss A	Yes, and the upshot of it is that they will support you and any other girl from this school who wants to play football. We can't have a team yet, unfortunately. We just don't have the facilities or the staff. But there is a County League and we think you should aim for one of the better teams, and Mr Williams has agreed to give you some coaching after school, once a week.
Charmian	Yeah!
Miss A	The thing is, Charmian, a lot of people have stuck their necks out for you. Everyone's going to be expecting great things. You can't let us down now.
Charmian	I won't, Miss, I promise.
Miss A	Good. Well, I look forward to seeing you in your first match.
Charmian	Thanks, Miss!
Gary	Great!
Charmian	(*surprised at hearing Gary*) What?
Miss A	You're not still here, are you, Gary?

Gary   Oops.

*He covers his mouth with his hands and tiptoes
away while they try not to laugh.*

Scene Twelve

*Characters: Girl Fans, Kingsley Boys' Fans, The
United Girls' Football Team (including Girl Players 1,
2 and 3), Charmian, Gary, Mr Williams, Terry
Thomson (United's Manager).*

*Charmian comes onto an empty stage in her light
blue football kit. She bounces around and practises
a few shots then she turns to the audience.*

Charmian   (*pointing to her kit*) Look at this! Never thought I'd
make it but I'm here. I'm in the top team in the
County League and I'm going to show them how it's
really done. We'll have won everything by the time
I've finished. It's great to be back. I haven't played
properly for ages but I've kept up with my practising
and I haven't lost any of my old skills. If anything I'm
sharper. Oh, it's going to be so brilliant!

*She runs off and the girl fans rush on stage waving
flags, scarves and banners chanting 'United for the
Cup', 'We want Charmian' and 'Charmian for
Champion'. Boy fans come on waving flags, scarves
and banners saying 'Kingsley for the Cup', 'We want
Scott' and 'Scott for Champion'. The two groups face
each other and chant and shout. Mr Williams, in
referee kit, rushes on and blows his whistle.*

Mr Williams   What on earth is going on here? That's enough all of
you! What are you boys doing here?

KB Fan 1	We've come to support Charmian, Sir.
Mr Williams	What, in the school's colours?
KB Fan 2	They're the only ones we've got, Sir.
Mr Williams	But this is the girls' team and they play in light blue.
Girl Fan 1	They're just trying to wind us up, Sir.
KB Fan 3	Come over here and say that.
Mr Williams	All right! That's enough, all of you. Now look, we're all here to support Charmian and her team so I don't want any trouble. Understood?
All	Yes, Sir.

He goes and they form a crowd at the back of the stage. Charmian comes on in a light blue strip with the other girls in her team. They jog about keeping warm and then the whistle blows. The football action could be mimed or a foam ball can be used. Not all of the team have to be on stage. Charmian tries to play but the others avoid her. She tries many times but cannot get the ball. She is jeered at. Then she stands still in the middle as they play around her. Suddenly the team stop in disappointment.

G Player 1	Oh, no! One against us.

They play again and the same happens. The boy fans heckle.

G Player 2	That's two against us!

Mr Williams blows for half time. The team go off.

KB Fan 1	Didn't think much of that. A bunch of daffodils could have played better.
KB Fan 2	Call herself a striker? She hasn't got a clue.
KB Fan 3	Well, what can you expect from a girl?
Girl Fan 2	Give her a chance. She's hardly had time to play yet.
KB Fan 3	Yeah, we noticed. She just stands around all the time.
KB Fan 1	Lead boots.

KB Fan 2	Yes, she's probably got her make-up bag and deodorant in them!

They laugh and jeer. The whistle blows for the second half. The team come back on. They play again. Charmian does not get to touch the ball. A third goal is scored against them. The boys heckle again.

KB Fans	(*chanting*) Go home, go home, go home, go home.
G Player 3	I don't believe it. Three-nil against us!

The final whistle blows. One by one the team, all except Charmian, go off heads down. Their supporters heckle them. The boys jeer the girls and Charmian.

KB Fan 2	Rubbish!
KB Fan 3	Useless!
KB Fan 1	You need our Scott.

Everybody goes offstage slowly, disgusted and disappointed. Charmian is alone. Terry Thomson, United's Manager, enters.

Manager	What the heck's going on, Charmian? You were worse than a lump of lard out there!
Charmian	No one would pass the ball to me, Terry.
Manager	Oh, so you were expecting everybody to run round fetching the ball for you, were you? Just expect it be handed to you on a plate?
Charmian	No.
Manager	Is that how you scored all those goals at junior school, was it, having the ball dropped at your feet in front of an open goal all the time?
Charmian	No, but they wouldn't let me have the ball any time.
Manager	That's just an excuse, girl. This is real football. We don't stand round gossiping all day and waiting for the ball to come to us. You go after it.
Charmian	Yes, Terry.

Manager   I don't know. You were supposed to be the best thing since sliced bread. A four-year-old could have done better! I dropped Donna for you and we've just lost our first match in ten games. If we'd have won we'd have set a new record. Think of that.

Charmian   I wasn't the only one in the team.

Manager   No, but let's put it this way. It's the first time you've played and it's the first time we've lost.

Charmian   It'll be different next time, Terry, I promise.

Manager   If there is a next time.

He goes. Charmian sits down, very unhappy. Gary enters, limping slightly. He hams it up when he sees Charmian.

Gary   Ooh, ooh, my leg!

He waits. She doesn't respond. He rolls over in mock agony trying to gain her attention. She still ignores him so he becomes serious.

Gary   What's up?

Charmian   It was terrible, Gary. My first game and I played really bad and we lost.

Gary   Well, it wasn't all your fault, was it?

Charmian   The manager thinks so.

Gary   Ah, don't take no notice of him. He's a right berk. Your first game's always like that.

Charmian   Did you have a bad first game?

Gary   No, I scored twice.

Charmian   Oh, thanks.

Gary   No, listen, right. That's unusual. Like, I always have to be different but everybody else I know had a bad first game. It's just nerves. So what happened?

Charmian   They wouldn't pass the ball to me, Gary. How can I play if I haven't got the ball?

Gary   Look, Char, you've got to play your own game. For yourself, I mean. You don't rely on nobody else. Just yourself. If you get the ball off the other team and your lot's in the way, chop their legs off.

Charmian   Gary!

Gary   No, seriously. Look after Number One. I promise you, if you start scoring they'll be all over you. They'll pass to you so many times you'll have to learn how to juggle. So next time –

Charmian   There isn't going to be a next time. The manager doesn't want me in the team any more.

Gary   Oh, come off it. You've only just got in. He's got to give you a better chance than that. I mean, I know managers, they might yell at you but they're fair.

Charmian   He wasn't fair to me.

Gary   That's 'cos he had no choice. You made him look daft. He'll be all right. All you've got to do is go out there and play. Show them, Char. You can do it!

Charmian   Are you sure, Gary?

Gary   Betcha. Now come on, it's grub time.

He gets up and then collapses, clutching his leg and moaning.

Charmian   (*very concerned*) Gary, Gary what's the matter? What's happened? Gary!

Gary   (*straightening up and smiling*) Nothing. Just testing.

Charmian   (*thumping him*) Gary!

He laughs and they go off.

Scene Thirteen

Characters: Charmian, Rina, Debbie, Karen, Emma, Miss Anderson.

The girls' changing room a few weeks later. It is empty. Charmian enters warily and looks round to see if anybody's there. She looks very unhappy. When she sees she's alone she sits down and puts her head in her hands. After a few moments she hears people coming so she hides. The girls rush in after Games. Emma flops down crossly.

Emma I tell you lot, I'm not doing Games any more. I hate it.

Debbie You have to, it's compulsory.

Emma Yeah, well I'll be away, or stay in the library or something.

Debbie Miss'll soon suss that one out. She always notices if you're missing.

Emma Then she'll just have to notice. I'm not going.

Karen I don't like Games either but I'm not skipping them.

Emma Oh, get you, little Miss Goody-Goody!

Karen Pass that sock, Debbie.

Debbie (*laughing*) Why? Do you want to stuff it down Emma's throat?

Emma Watch it!

Rina Did anyone see that programme on the telly last night about that virus that eats you up inside?

Debbie Ugh, no. Sounds disgusting.

Emma I watched *Emmerdale*, then *The Bill*, then *Brookside*.

Rina Don't you get fed up with all those soaps?

Emma	No, I like them. And *Coronation Street* and *Home and Away* and –
Debbie	(*cutting her off*) Tell us more about this horrible virus thing, Rina.
Rina	Well, apparently it's really infectious and once you've got it there's nothing they can do. It turns your insides to jelly and you die.
Debbie	Ugh!
Emma	Are we going to get it?
Rina	No, it's not in this country.
Debbie	Yet.
Emma	What do you want to watch things like that for? It's enough to frighten you to death.
Rina	I found it quite interesting. I want to be a doctor so I need to know about these things.
Emma	I want to be a model.
Karen	We know. You never stop telling us.
Debbie	You'll be all right, then, you don't have to know anything to be that.

Miss Anderson comes in. They quickly start changing.

Miss A	I might have known it would be you lot wasting time again. Come on, girls, get on with it; you've got Art next. Has anyone seen Charmian?
Debbie	She's practising her football, Miss.
Miss A	Well, when she gets back tell her I want to see her straight away, OK?
Debbie	Yes, Miss.

Miss Anderson goes.

Debbie	Mm, wonder what Char's done? Miss didn't look too pleased.
Emma	Messed up that girls' football team again, I bet. All that rubbish about how marvellous she was. Ever since she's been in it they've lost every match.

Debbie	Shut up, Emma. It's not her fault. It's the others. They won't let her play properly. They're too jealous of her. They know she'll show them all up if she gets a real chance.
Emma	That's just an excuse. If she was that good she'd have done something by now. She's been in it weeks.
Debbie	Whose side are you on anyway?
Emma	Come on, she's rubbish and you know it. I mean, all that showing off about how good she was. Now she's really been shown up.
Debbie	I thought you were supposed to be her friend.
Emma	Not any more. She's pathetic. She's just so sad.
Debbie	Fine friend you are!
Emma	It's none of your business so you can shut up. So there.
Karen	(*looking at her watch*) Look at the time. Mr MacDonald will kill us. Come on!

They hurry off. When they are gone Charmian comes out from where she's been hiding and looks round carefully before running off.

Scene Fourteen

Characters: Miss Anderson, Mr Williams.
Miss Anderson hurries after Mr Williams.

Miss A	Mervyn! Mervyn, hang on a minute, please!
Mr Williams	Where's the fire, Linda?
Miss A	Have you seen Charmian King today?

Mr Williams	Nope, didn't see her yesterday either and she was supposed to have a coaching session with me after school. Didn't bother to tell me she wasn't going to turn up, did she? She's a dead loss, if you ask me, Linda. All that fuss made about her and what's she done, eh? Nothing, that's what.
Miss A	Mervyn, this is a bit more serious than your coaching lesson. It looks as though she's gone missing.
Mr Williams	Missing?
Miss A	Yes, she hasn't been seen by anybody in school since yesterday lunch time. Her parents thought she stayed overnight with a friend but when she didn't turn up after school today her mother checked with the friend and then rang us straight away.
Mr Williams	Oh, that's bad.
Miss A	Yes, I think all this pressure about the football has got to her.
Mr Williams	What's happening then?
Miss A	Well, the police have been informed and they are looking for her but they're going to give it until tomorrow morning and if she hasn't been found by then they'll mount a full-scale search and go public, announce it on the news and so on.
Mr Williams	Blooming heck! Do you think I was –
Miss A	No, I don't think anyone's to blame, as such, not even Charmian herself. It's all got a bit too much for her and she's taken off. She's probably staying somewhere close and will soon get fed up and go home.
Mr Williams	They don't think she's . . . ah . . . that someone has . . .
Miss A	Abducted her? No, not at this stage. Apparently, she's taken off once or twice before when she's had a row with her mum, or didn't like school, and she's always come home again after a day or two. That's what they think's happened this time.

| **Mr Williams** | Thank heavens for that. Well, I'll keep my eyes peeled, Linda. |
| **Miss A** | Thanks, Mervyn. |

Scene Fifteen

Characters: Karen, Rina, Debbie, Emma.

The next morning at school. Rina, Karen and Debbie are talking before registration. Emma enters.

Debbie	Watch it. Look who's just walked in.
Emma	Here, have you lot heard? Charmian King's run away.
Karen	We know. So what?
Emma	Well, I'm not surprised, I wouldn't want to show my face if I was her.
Karen	Don't be so bitchy, Emma. This is serious.
Debbie	Yes, she hasn't been seen since lunch break on Tuesday.
Emma	What do you expect me to do about it?
Debbie	You could be a bit more concerned. You're supposed to be her friend.
Emma	Where do you reckon she's got to then?
Debbie	I don't know.
Emma	You must have some idea.
Rina	No, we haven't. If we did we'd let the teachers know. Anyway, Miss Anderson wanted to see us after school about it yesterday but we don't know anything. Char never told anyone she was going.
Emma	She's got herself into right trouble over this, I bet.
Debbie	Well, don't sound so pleased about it.

Emma   I'm not.

Karen Yes, you are. You're always on about her.

Emma   No, I'm not.

Debbie Liar. You couldn't wait for her to fall flat on her face in football, could you?

Emma   Look, I don't have to stay here and listen to you going on like this.

Debbie No, you don't so why don't you get lost?

Emma   Right, I'll go and talk to somebody else then.

Debbie Good and don't forget to spread it all round the school about Char, will you?

Emma makes a face at Debbie and stalks off.

Debbie She really gets up my nose sometimes.

Rina   Don't let it bother you, she's not worth it.

Debbie Yeah, I wouldn't mind but I bet as soon as Charmian's back and starts playing well and getting all the publicity and that, Emma'll be back saying what a great friend she is.

Karen Don't worry, Charmian can see through her.

Rina   It's awful, though, isn't it? Going off like that. She must be really stressed out. Poor Charmian.

Debbie Yes, and I bet her mum and dad are going spare. Mine would.

Rina   Mine too. You don't think – I mean, you don't think something's happened to her, do you?

Debbie What, like someone's taken her or something?

Rina   (*worried*) Yes.

Debbie I don't know. I don't want to think about it.

Karen Nor me.

Rina   She's run away before though, hasn't she?

Debbie Yeah, she went off a couple of times when we were at the juniors. I bet she's done the same this time. (*upset*) Oh, Rina, she's got to have.

Rina   It'll be all right, don't worry.

Karen   Yes, come on, don't get all upset. You know what Char's like. Knowing her, she's probably having a great time somewhere. (*pause*) Look, there's Gary. Bet he knows something. Let's go and see him. Hey, Gary!

They hurry off.

Scene Sixteen

Characters: Charmian, Gary.

It is later that day and dark. Charmian is hanging around the school cold and hungry. She sits huddled in a doorway. She shivers and moans a couple of times and keeps looking around as though expecting someone. Gary appears.

Charmian   You took your time.

Gary   I've been looking everywhere for you. I thought you said you'd be round the back of the Arts block.

Charmian   No, you idiot, that was last night. I told you I could be seen there from the houses opposite.

Gary   Oh, yeah, I forgot. Here, my mum never noticed you slept in our shed last night.

Charmian   Yes, and blooming uncomfortable it was too and it stank in there.

Gary   Better than being out in the cold though?

Charmian   Only just. You got that stuff?

Gary   Here it is.

Gary hands her a carrier bag. She dives into it and brings out some food and drink.

Gary	I lifted the sandwiches and chocolate from the newsagent's but the Coke's mine from break.
Charmian	Thanks, Gary, but you shouldn't have nicked anything. You might have got caught.
Gary	Nah, he's a right berk in there. Anyway, apart from just this once I don't do that any more. It's a mug's game. Anyhow, I'd lose my place in the team if I got caught. It's not worth it. (*pause as Charmian eats and drinks*) Listen, Char, right. Don't you think it's about time you went home now? Like, you've made your point and that –
Charmian	No, Gary!
Gary	Listen up, right. It's freezing out here, you haven't eaten properly, you've got nowhere proper to sleep and your mum and dad are going spare.
Charmian	I can't, Gary, not yet.
Gary	I'll come with you.
Charmian	No!
Gary	I'll take the blame. I'll tell them it was my idea.
Charmian	(*throwing her food down and moving away*) Will you shut up, Gary! You're just the same as them, always on at me. Always thinking I'm a right idiot. I hate it! Just go away and leave me alone.
Gary	Char, I'm sorry –
Charmian	It's always Carlton this and Charlene that. All their cups and medals and things, and what have I got? Nothing. And they're good at school, top marks and everything and Mum and Dad never stop telling me how lazy I am and how hard they work. But I do. I work really hard but I just can't do as well as them and all the teachers hate me. Everyone goes on and on. I can't take it any more, Gary. I'm never going back.
Gary	Come on, Char, don't say that. It's not like that really. Come on, you ought to go home now.

Charmian	No, and if you grass me up –
Gary	I wouldn't do that, Char, you know I wouldn't but . . . (*pause*) Shall we go, then?
Charmian	I am not going home. Ever!! Got that?
Gary	OK, OK, I'm not going to make you but you can't stay here. Let's go.
Charmian	You mean, to your poxy shed again?
Gary	You got any other suggestions?
Charmian	No.
Gary	Well then, let's go.

He gathers up the food bag and they go.

Scene Seventeen

Characters: Mr King, Mrs King, Charlene, Woman Police Constable.

Mrs King is sitting down very distressed. Charlene is trying to help her.

Mrs King	It's been three days now, three days.
Charlene	Look, Mum, she's done this before and she's come back every time.
Mrs King	But this is different. I know it, I feel it in my bones. She's been so funny lately, acting all strange. Oh, Lord, what's she been and done, eh?
Charlene	Nothing, Mum. I told you, it'll be like last time, remember? She was staying with Uncle Robert and he thought we knew. What do you bet she's done the same thing this time?

Mrs King	But I rang Robert and he's said she hadn't been near his place and I know he was telling the truth.
Charlene	Well, she won't have gone there again. She's too clever for that. She'll know that's the first place we'd look after last time. Oh, I could kill her for this! Hasn't she caused you enough trouble already?
Mrs King	She's just a baby. (*getting upset again*) Oh, who's got my baby? Who's taken my baby!
Charlene	Mum, it's OK, it's going to be all right, I promise you.
Mr King	(*calling off*) Hi, honey, I'm home.
	Mr King enters.
Mr King	(*seeing his wife upset*) Oh, Grace, Grace, what's happened, darling?
Charlene	(*moving so that Mr King can sit next to Mrs King*) Nothing, Dad. We haven't heard anything. Mum's just upset.
Mr King	Oh, honey, don't you go getting yourself into this state. She's going to come home when she gets too cold and hungry. You'll see.
	The doorbell rings.
Charlene	I'll go.
	She goes out and returns with a policewoman.
Charlene	(*fearfully indicating the policewoman*) Mum, Dad.
WPC	Mr and Mrs King, may I have a word with you?
	Mrs King screams and falls into Mr King's arms.

Scene Eighteen

Characters: Gary, Charmian, Miss Anderson,
Mr King, Mrs King.

The gym the next evening. It is late and dark outside
and only street lamps light the gym through the
windows high up near the roof. Charmian enters
warily and when she sees it's empty she switches
on the light. Then she fetches a ball and starts
practising her football skills but she cannot do
anything right. She is tired and hungry but won't
give in. She hears a door bang and moves to one
side. Gary enters.

Gary	(*whispering*) Char, Char, you there?
Charmian	Oh, it's you. You nearly frightened the life out of me.
Gary	You knew I was coming. I got that chocolate and stuff you wanted.
Charmian	(*resuming her practice*) Thanks.
Gary	Look, don't you think you ought to let your mum and dad know you're all right now?
Charmian	I'm not going home yet, Gary, so don't keep trying to make me.
Gary	Why not?
Charmian	Because they'll only keep on at me and I've got to get my game right.
Gary	Look, you can't stay away for ever. I mean, I'll get into dead trouble when they find out I know where you are and have been helping you and haven't told them.
Charmian	(*angrily*) You'd better get lost then! Don't want to get you into any trouble, do we?
Gary	Char, don't get stressed. I'm only trying to help.
Charmian	Well, you're not. OK?

Gary	Char, don't take it out on me. It's not my fault.
Charmian	Get lost, Gary, you're a right drag. I don't want you hanging round any more.

He is hurt by this but waits for her to change her mind. She ignores him and carries on practising. He is about to go when he hears a door bang. He is really startled by this and panics.

Gary	Somebody's coming!

He looks around and then dives into the office. Charmian ignores the approaching footsteps. Miss Anderson enters.

Miss A	Charmian!! It's you. Whatever are you doing in here?
Charmian	Practising. I've got to get it right, Miss.
Miss A	Do you realise how worried people are about you? Your parents are beside themselves with worry. The police are looking for you. Where've you been all this time?
Charmian	Just around.
Miss A	And you shouldn't be in this gym. It should be locked at this time of night. How did you get in?
Charmian	(*she shoots at goal and misses*) See. It's useless. I'm no good any more.
Miss A	I'd like some answers to my questions!
Charmian	I can't think why I thought I'd be good enough for United's team. I can't even hit a 30-foot wall from two feet away.
Miss A	Now come on, stop all this nonsense and come and sit down.

Charmian ignores her.

Miss A	Charmian, I mean what I say!
Charmian	(*getting very angry and screaming*) Get off my back, will you! You're just the same as all the rest. Always going on at me. Always having a go. I've had enough. You're all the same. Calling me names,

laughing at me. I'm not going home, I'm not coming back to school, and I'm not playing for that stupid team again either! Not ever. So you can all go and take a running jump!!

She runs to the wall and bangs her fists against it in rage and frustration. She is close to breaking point. Miss Anderson goes across to her and speaks gently.

Miss A   Charmian, I know how it is for you right now but acting like this isn't going to help, you know. You're exhausted, you're cold and hungry, and you want to go home, whatever you say, but you're frightened about what your parents are going to do and what the school is going to say and having to face all your friends again – but nothing is ever as bad as you think it is. Come on, I promise you, you won't get into any trouble over this but you've got to agree to calm down and talk it over and then let me arrange for your parents to come and take you home.

Charmian   No! I'm not going back. They think I'm an idiot. Everybody thinks I've ruined the team.

Miss A   No, they don't. They're all behind you. They want you to do well but sometimes things aren't that easy. But you can't run away at the first sign of trouble. Come and sit down and talk it over. (*she waits and Charmian makes a move*) That's better. Now come and sit down and tell me what this is all about.

They sit down.

Charmian   There's nothing to tell. I've lost it, that's all. And I'm never going to get it back, and Terry our manager's really mad at me for ruining the team and losing all those matches. And the others hate me and everyone else is laughing at me. I've had enough and I just feel like running away for ever and never coming back.

Miss A   We all feel like that sometimes but running away's not going to solve anything. All it does is cause a lot of heartache for everybody, especially your family. Just think what's been going through your mum and dad's minds.

Charmian I can't do anything right, it's hopeless.

Miss A Now listen to me, I didn't fight for your place in the best girls' team around just to have you throw it all away because things aren't going right for you at the moment. You represent me and all the girls in this school and all the other schools with girls who want to play football. Let me tell you something straight, Charmian King, I'm not going to have you letting us down.

Charmian It's not that easy, Miss. I can't play right at the moment.

Miss A Everybody goes through bad patches. You get off form and it's really awful and then suddenly it's all back again and you're playing brilliantly. Believe me, it happens to all footballers, even the top ones. It's nothing unusual.

Charmian Yes, but I haven't even had a chance, have I? Nobody's seen me play like I used to. They think I was just showing off and I'm a rubbish player from the start. They don't want me and that's that.

Miss A I know that's how it feels at the moment but give them time and you'll see. They'll soon get used to you. They'll forget you're even there and once you start scoring they won't ignore you then.

Charmian I don't think I'll get another chance to do anything. I'm sure Mr Thomson's going to drop me from the next match, and all the other ones after that probably.

Miss A Well, let's cross that bridge when we come to it, OK? But right now we have to let your parents and the police know that you're safe.

Charmian (*giving in at last*) OK.

Miss A   Good. You stay here – no running off, mind – and I'll go into the office and make those phone calls.

Charmian   Uh, Miss, can't you phone from the staffroom?

Miss A   No, why?

Charmian   Because . . .

Gary appears from the Games Office eating a chocolate bar and a packet of crisps.

Miss A   Gary Greene! I might have known you'd be involved. What are you doing here?

Gary   I came here to give Charmian some chocolate and stuff.

Miss A   And eating it yourself, I see. Gary, you're a damned menace! Do you mean to tell me that you've known where Charmian's been all along and you didn't tell anyone?

Gary   No, Miss. I mean, yes, Miss, I did know but she wouldn't let me tell anyone. She'd have duffed me up if I had.

Charmian   He's right, Miss, I would have.

Miss A   Do you know how worried Charmian's mum and dad have been?

Charmian   It was my fault, Miss, I wouldn't let him tell. He wanted to.

Miss A   (*sighing*) I don't know. What am I going to do with you pair? Look, I have to go and phone. Stay here, both of you, and don't move till I get back.

She goes into the office. Gary sits next to Charmian who bursts into tears.

Gary   It's going to be all right, Char. Nobody'll get on at you. They'll be so pleased to see you're all right that they won't bother, that's the truth. All right? Now, listen up, I think I know what's wrong with your game.

Charmian   (*through her tears*) Oh, yes?

Gary	Like, it's a question of confidence really.
Charmian	Confidence?
Gary	Yeah, you don't believe in yourself any more.
Charmian	It's not that. I can't kick any more. I can't pass. I can't shoot.
Gary	Yeah, like I said it's all down to confidence. Once you lose that everything goes.
Charmian	How come?
Gary	Well, I think it was all that hype and stuff and everyone was expecting you to be so brilliant and in the end you couldn't hack it.
Charmian	Are you saying I'm chicken?
Gary	No, it was all the pressure. I'd be just the same.
Charmian	So what can I do then?
Gary	First you've got to relax and stop thinking you've got to score 20 goals every game. Strikers don't just whack the ball in the back of the net. They've got to know when to make runs and when to hang back, and when to make passes and when to hold the ball up, and when not to be selfish and when to pass the ball and let another player score.
Charmian	Right.
Gary	And when to say thanks to the best player in the world.
Charmian	(*whacking him*) Gary!

Miss Anderson returns.

Miss A	Your parents are on their way, Charmian, and the police will want to talk to you in the morning but it's just a chat, you're not in any trouble.
Charmian	Thanks, Miss. How was Mum and Dad?
Miss A	Very relieved. Your mum burst into tears but she says you're not to worry and your dad said not to worry too because he's packing you off on the first plane to Grenada tomorrow.

Charmian   (*smiling*) Yeah, that sounds like him. He didn't mean it though, did he?

Miss A   No, of course not. He's just so pleased you're all right. He sounds a nice man, your dad.

Charmian   Yeah, he's really great.

Miss A   Now, once everything's back to normal you're going to need to get yourself sorted out. No more running away and no more flogging yourself to death late at night in gyms, because none of it's doing you any good, is it?

Charmian   No, Miss.

Miss A   And you're not improving, just getting tired out. So when you get home watch television and relax. Have a few days off and forget about football, and when you next play go after them and get that ball and show them that you are just as good, even better, than they are. Don't wait for the ball to be given to you. Tackle, go for it and score! OK? But be part of the team as well. That's very important.

Charmian   That's what Gary said.

Miss A   Well, occasionally he speaks some sense.

Gary   Thanks for those few kind words, Miss. Cor, I'm well hungry.

Charmian   How can you be? You've eaten all my stuff.

Gary   Should have had my tea ages ago.

Miss A   (*fishes in her bag and takes out a roll*) Here, have this. I didn't get time to eat it at lunch.

Gary takes it gratefully and stuffs most of it in his mouth in one go.

Miss A   Come on, let's lock up here and get out to the front gate where I said we'd meet Charmian's parents.

Gary   Can I have a lift home, Char?

Charmian   All right, I think you've just about earned it.

Gary   Aw, some people are never satisfied.

The lights dim as they walk off. Lights up as Mr and Mrs King enter.

Mrs King   Where are they? Miss Anderson said they'd meet us here.

Mr King   (*checking his watch*) We got here a bit quicker than we said.

Mrs King   Only because you drove like a maniac.

Mr King   No, I did not. Anyway, I just wanted to get here. I don't want her to go changing her mind and running off again.

Mrs King   Miss Anderson won't let her – (*unsure*) – will she?

Mr King   Of course not. She knows how worried we've been.

Mrs King   Oh, when I get hold of that girl –

Mr King   Now, honey, we don't want to go laying into her before she's even back home. Give her time and then she can explain herself.

Mrs King   Oh, the trouble she's caused us!

Mr King   I know, I know, but she's been through it too. We've got to remember that. Kids don't run away for nothing.

Mrs King   (*angry*) What are you talking about? She's got a good home. She doesn't lack for anything. What does she want to go running away for? I've been out of my mind.

Mr King   I don't think it's anything to do with us, honey. It's all that football business. But once you've run away it's quite hard to come back. You've got to face the music and you've got to say you're sorry. That can be very difficult.

Mrs King   We'd have got a good hiding when I was a child if we'd done anything like this.

Mr King   I know but it's different these days and now we've got her back we have to tread carefully – and hear her side of the story.

Mrs King   But –

Mr King   And give her time and –

Mrs King   Oh, hush. I think that's her.

Charmian runs onto the stage and into her mother's arms. Gary and Miss Anderson follow on.

Mrs King   Oh, where you been, child? I've been beside myself with worry!

Charmian   (*tearful*) Oh, Mum, I'm so sorry. Are you really mad at me?

Mr King   No, honey, we're just glad you're safe and back with us.

They all hug each other, joyful and relieved.

Gary   Cor, what a fuss! Anybody'd think she'd run away or something.

Scene Nineteen

Characters: United Girls' Football Team including Charmian, The Opposing Girls' Team from Borough Park, Referee, Terry Thomson (United's Manager), Mr Williams, Miss Anderson, Gary, Georgina, Pushpa, Kelly, Ali, Conroy, Karen, Debbie, Rina, United Fans, Borough Fans.

Everybody but the team players comes on stage. The two groups of fans stand opposite each other. They warm up with songs, clapping and chanting. They sing to the tune of 'Glory, Glory Alleluia'.

United Fans   Glory, glory, our United! Glory, glory our United. Glory, glory our United and we all go marching on.

Boro' Fans   Glory, glory Borough Park! Glory, glory Borough Park. Glory, glory Borough Park and we all go marching on.

They clap.

United Fans   She's fat, she's round, she'll score in any ground.

Boro' Fans   She's fat, she's round, she hasn't scored in any ground.

They clap, then sing to the tune of 'Three Lions'.

United Fans   She's coming home, she's coming home, she's coming, Charmian's coming home.

Boro' Fans   She's going home, she's going home, she's going, King is going home.

They wave their scarves and rattles and cheer, then chant.

United Fans   Terry Thomson's light blue army. Terry Thomson's light blue army.

Boro' Fans   Terry Thomson's stupid army. Terry Thomson's stupid army.

They clap in unison again and then break out into ordinary clapping and cheering as Charmian's team run on and warm up to loud cheers, boos and whistling. They go offstage. Borough Park come on to their supporters' cheers and United's boos and whistling. They go off. The referee comes prancing on looking important, running on the spot and so on. He checks his whistle, book and watch. They chant at him.

All   The referee is stupid! The referee is stupid!

Then he stands still and makes movements that indicate he is starting the game. He blows his whistle and runs offstage and they all shout after him. Then they move to the front of the stage and look out at the audience as though the match is going on there. As people talk the crowd reacts to the play but not so loud that the dialogue cannot be heard.

Ali	Come on the Borough.
Gary	Come on United.
Karen	Do you think they'll win, Gary?
Gary	Course they will, but it'll be close.
Conroy	Not with that useless girl from your school, mate. What's her name? King.
Gary	Watch it.
Rina	Leave it, Gary, we don't want any trouble.
All	Ooh!
Conroy	Close.
Gary	Yah, miles away.
Georgina	You've got to admit, though, she's rubbish and she kept telling everyone she was so brilliant.
Gary	Give her a chance. It's tough at the top.
Conroy	What would you know about it?
Rina	That's Gary Greene you're talking to.
Conroy	Oh, sorry, mate – top striker in the schools' league, yeah?
Gary	That's me. Mr Wonderful.
Ali	Aw, come on, Ref. No way!
	They watch the match and comment on the action encouraging their teams. Then the Borough fans roar and United's supporters show their disappointment.
Conroy	Yesss! Goal!
Karen	Oh, no.
Gary	Lucky.
Pushpa	Come on the Borough.
Ali	Easy. Easy.
Boro' Fans	One-nil, one-nil, one-nil, one-nil.
	The crowd watch the match and react to what is going on then the excitement builds.
Debbie	Come on, United.

Georgina	You're wasting your breath. They've got lead boots, your lot.
Debbie	That ref's biased. He keeps awarding your lot free kicks.
Georgina	That's because your lot's fouling all the time. They can't get the ball midfield so they get our players instead.
Gary	Just you watch this. That's it, Char, go on, go on, pass it, go on. (*disappointed*) Oh!
Georgina	Told you.
Gary	She'll score in a minute, don't you worry.
Pushpa	We're not. She isn't going to score.
Karen	Oh no? Well, watch this. Come on, Char.
Gary	Round one, round two. That's it, girl. Now go on, keep going and pass it to the number ten.
Debbie	Shoot, Char!
Gary	No, she don't stand a chance from there. She's got to pass it. Go on, girl, remember what I told you, pass it. That's it. Great. Now come on, Ten, shoot. Yess!!
Debbie	Goal!
	United's supporters erupt as a goal is scored.
Karen	Equaliser!
Gary	Right on half time.
Ali	Yeah, but your wondergirl didn't score yet again, did she?
Gary	No, but she made the goal. Did you see that run? Half the park, mate – and past half your team.
Ali	Anybody could've done that.
Rina	Don't kid yourself. Gary knows what he's talking about.
United Fans	One more, one more, one more, one more.
Boro' Fans	No chance, no chance, no chance, no chance.

*A whistle blows. The fans move positions and talk
among themselves. Lights dim. Lights up and the
fans settle down to watch the second half. The
referee runs on, blows his whistle and runs off. The
fans move to the front of the stage and cheer.*

Gary   Second half. Here we go.

United Fans   Come on, United.

Boro' Fans   Come on the Borough. One more, one more, one
more, one more.

United Fans   No more, no more, no more, no more.

*They watch the action and comment on
what's happening.*

Gary   No chance! Oi, ref, are you blind or something? (*to
Rina*) Did you see that?

Rina   Yes, she was deliberately tripped.

Gary   Penalty, ref.

Ali   She took a dive.

Gary   Never.

Ali   Come off it. She could have gone in the deep end of
a swimming pool with that dive.

Gary   Are you calling Charmian a cheat?

Ali   Yes, as a matter of fact I am. What are you going to
do about it, mate?

Gary   Right –

Rina   (*restraining him*) Leave it, Gary. They'll chuck
you out and then you won't see the rest of
the match.

*He grumbles but continues to watch the match
peacefully. The Borough supporters groan in
disappointment. Then the United supporters get
excited and encourage their players as the ball goes
upfield, and they too groan as a shot goes wide.*

Karen   What's the time?

Debbie	There's about five minutes left.
Karen	Come on, come on.
Georgina	It's going to be a draw. Either that or we'll score the winner.
Gary	Who says?
Rina	We've got to score again.
Gary	Don't worry, we will.
Debbie	Look at this. It's Charmian. I think she's going to score.
	They shout at her.
Pushpa	Doubt it. We haven't lost a final yet.
	All the United supporters start screaming for Charmian to score, then they calm down as Borough get the ball.
Conroy	Yo, not this time.
Georgina	That's it, Marlene, get them. Come on.
Conroy	We've still got a chance to win. Tackle, Sophie, tackle!
Ali	Great. Come on, Borough.
Georgina	Oh, no.
Karen	We've got it back. Come on!
Gary	That's it, Julie, go on, keep going, pass. Pass, you idiot. Pass it to Charmian.
Debbie	She's got it now. Come on, Char. Come on.
Rina	I think she's going to score.
Conroy	No chance, our keeper's too good.
Gary	Not for our Charmian. Shoot, Char!!
United Fans	Yess!!
Boro' Fans	(*groaning with disappointment*) No!
Karen	Did you see that? Brilliant, right over the keeper's head.
Rina	We're in front, Gary.

Gary   Yeah, and there's only a few minutes left.

He gives Rina a hug. She can't believe it and looks at him all starry-eyed but he has eyes only for the game.

Gary   Great one, Char.

Karen   Who says she's rubbish now?

Gary   Oi, ref! No way.

Karen   What's going on?

Ali   Vicious tackle from King.

Debbie   It wasn't her fault. Your defender tried to elbow her in the throat.

Pushpa   Never touched her.

Karen   Yes, she did, we saw it.

Georgina It's a red card. She's being sent off!

Debbie   That's not fair.

Conroy   It's what she deserves, clogging at our players.

Rina   That ref's biased. He's for the other team.

Gary   (*shouting*) Oi, no way, ref!

Debbie   Unfair!

Kelly   Rubbish. She got what she deserved. Only ten of them now, Borough, come on!

United fans jeer and boo at the referee. Play goes on. Lights dim as the fans move to the back of the stage and freeze. Lights up on Charmian as she walks on and sits dejectedly at the front of the stage. Terry Thomson enters. She braces herself for his comments.

Charmian I'm sorry, Terry, I didn't mean to kick her but she'd been on at me the whole game and it was just the last straw and all right I lost my rag but, I mean, she really deserved it.

Manager   It's OK, Charmian, I haven't come to have a go. As a matter of fact I thought the ref's decision was

	terrible. I saw what that Borough player was up to the whole match and I intend to lodge a complaint. So don't you worry.
Charmian	Really, Terry?
Manager	Oh, yes. Disgraceful, it was and you should have had a penalty but never mind, I think we're about to win this one and it's all down to you, girl.
Charmian	Me?
Manager	Yes, you played above yourself, girl. You played them off the park! You set up the first goal and scored the winner. The game's nearly over and it doesn't look like anyone else is going to score. We've won the League Cup, girl. So you can play, after all.
Charmian	Yeah, maybe.
Manager	No 'maybes', love. You were the business today. Well done. Never thought I'd see it but I have to say you did well.
Charmian	Straight up, Terry?
Manager	Oh, no doubt about it. Like a demon, you were. You showed them, eh?
Charmian	(*surprised*) Yes, suppose I did.
	There is a long whistle blow and lights up briefly on the crowd as they roar then lights down as they freeze again.
Manager	That's it. Sounds like it's all over and we've won.
Charmian	(*very relieved*) Oh, great.
Manager	Come on, girl, let's get that Cup in our hands and then go and celebrate.
	Miss Anderson and Mr Williams enter.
Miss A	Well done, Charmian, that was a fantastic performance.
Mr Williams	Great stuff, King.
Charmian	Thank you, Miss, Sir.

Miss A Told you, didn't I?

Charmian And you were right.

Manager (*getting impatient*) Come on, come on, let's get out there and celebrate. We've got a Cup to collect.

Charmian needs no further encouragement. She runs off cheering. The others laugh and follow her off. Lights up on the fans who break and start to celebrate. The Cup is paraded. Charmian enters. They cheer and lift her up on their shoulders. Gary steps forward and calls for silence.

Gary Quiet, you lot! (*to the audience*) Right everybody before you go home we want you to do a Mexican wave and join in the singing. The front row has to stand up and wave, then the second row, and so on to the back and then to the front again – and if you don't do it properly I'll set Charmian on you. And when you've done that we want some of you to join us on the stage and sing 'You'll Never Walk Alone'. Then you can go home and we can have our party to celebrate.

Gary oversees the Mexican wave in the audience and then he invites some onto the stage. Everyone, including the audience, sings 'You'll Never Walk Alone'.

The End

Hoping for Charlie

Notes: Hoping for Charlie

The first year at senior boarding school begins in the Third Year (Year Nine). Pupils belong to a particular House and sleep in dormitories (dorms) of about five to seven people with a prefect to look after them. Each House has a House Mistress or Master in charge. A matron is there to see to the laundry, and is often a mother figure to the pupils. What follows is a fairly typical day.

7.30am – Wake Up: Third Years on 'Wake Up Duty' have to get up early and wake up the whole House by ringing a bell. They would leave the Upper Sixth (Year Thirteen) till last.

7.30–8.20am – Breakfast: You might have to walk in all weathers to another building to get to the Dining Hall. Breakfast may be cereals, toast, sausage, bacon, waffles, coffee or tea. Some prefects get you to bring them breakfast, which means creeping out of the Dining Hall with the food, hoping you aren't seen.

8.30–9am – Chapel or Assembly: Chapel for a religious service every day including Saturday and Sunday, unless there's an Assembly for House or School. A Third Year rings the chapel bell to summon everybody, usually swinging on the bell ropes. You can't miss Chapel as a register is taken.

9am–1pm – Lessons: You have lessons all morning with a short break. Boarding schools are very big and you move from block to block for lessons.

1–2.30pm – Lunch: In the Dining Hall; free time afterwards.

2.30–6pm – Winter: On Mondays, Wednesdays and Fridays there are Games then lessons. On Tuesdays and Thursdays you have activities such as art, chess, computer club, languages and then lessons.

2.30–6pm – Summer: Lessons first then Games or activities.

6–7pm – Tea: This is the last meal of the day provided by the school. If you want anything else you get it yourself in the cookhole (a small kitchen for pupils) or if you're a Senior you go to the local take-away.

7.15–9pm – Prep: This is homework and is compulsory and supervised. After prep you can watch TV, visit friends in other Houses or whatever (if you're not gated – a punishment, which means you have to stay in your House during free time).

10pm – Bedtime: All Third Years are expected to be in bed by 10pm.

List of Characters

Boys
Charlie Massingham
Ben Russell
Hugo de la Haye
Femi Adegboye
Robert Chang
Prefect
Sixth Former
Boys from the House

Girls
Catherine
Emily
Laura
Frances

Adults
Mr Vaughan, Head of House
Mr Appleyard, Head Master (Mr A)
Dr O'Donnell, Consultant (O'Donnell)
Ms Haden, Registrar
Mr Singh, House Doctor
Miss Johnson, Medical Student
Miss Kumani, Medical Student
Mr Young, Medical Student
Rachel, Charlie's mother
Julian, Charlie's father
Paolo, Rachel's boyfriend
Derek Higginbotham
School Nurse
Louise, a Nurse
Vera, a Staff Nurse
Night Nurse
Sister

Hoping for Charlie

ACT ONE

Scene One

Characters: Ben, Hugo, Charlie.

The old stable block courtyard where a group of Third Year boys are playing football. Charlie limps around and after a while drops out.

Ben Over to me, Hugo.

Hugo That's it. Right, shoot!

Charlie Shoot, Ben!

Ben lets fly and the ball cannons into a statue. The head is knocked off and rolls around. Everyone freezes for a moment.

Charlie Ben, you idiot, you've knocked Joshua Perkins' block off! What are we going to do now?

Hugo What do you mean 'we'? He did it. I'm not copping it for him.

Charlie Oh, come on, de la Haye, you were playing same as us.

Hugo So what? It wasn't me who broke the stupid statue. Froggy'll go ape when he finds out. This is out of bounds to Thirds. I'm out of here.

Ben Go on then, but you grass and there'll be trouble.

Hugo I'm not going to grass but I'm not taking the blame either. See you.

Hugo goes. Charlie stands forlornly holding the offending football.

Ben Don't worry, Charlie, de la Haye won't say anything but I think we'd better get out of here before someone sees us.

They run off round the back of the stable block where they crouch behind some large aluminium bins and Ben bursts out laughing.

Ben Hey, that was really something!

Charlie It's not funny, Ben. Hugo's right, Froggy will go ballistic when he finds out.

Ben He won't know it's us. It could be anybody from any House.

Charlie Bet Hugo grasses.

Ben He'd better not or I'll get him. (*laughing again*) But I was creasing up. You should have seen your face and I swear old Perkins looked a bit surprised too!

Charlie It's a crummy statue anyway. I hate it. Some stupid kid who died years ago. What did he want to go and die for? Nobody knows him any more. Yuk, that girlie coat and that stupid smirk.

Ben Not now I've wiped the smile off his face. Anyway, who cares? He's been dead for centuries. He'll be nothing but a skeleton by now. (*singing*) 'Dem bones, dem bones, dem dry bones!'

Charlie Yeah, you're right. Who cares? He certainly doesn't. He'll be all eaten by worms and maggots by now.

Ben We'll be like that one day.

Charlie No way. I'm not being buried, I'm being cremated.

Ben (*putting on a vicar's voice*) Ashes to ashes. Dust to dust.

Charlie Talking of ash. You got any fags?

Ben Yes, hold on.

Charlie Great, 'cos I'm dying for one. Better look out for the prefects and old Froggy though.

Ben No chance. They'll never find us here. They can't be bothered, it's too far for them to walk.

Scene Two

*Characters: Ben, Charlie, Hugo, Head of House
Mr Vaughan, Prefect, Boys from the House.*

*There is a House meeting in the Junior Common
Room. Everyone in the House must attend. Charlie,
Ben and Hugo are at the back trying not to be seen.
The Head of House, Frank Vaughan, nicknamed
Froggy, is addressing the boys.*

Mr Vaughan   And finally, the not inconsiderable matter of the
Quad statue of Joshua Perkins, a boy from this
school who died so tragically at the age of thirteen
when he fell off his horse . . .

The boys snigger.

Charlie   Stupid kid. I'm going to enjoy myself, be famous,
have fun.

Hugo   Oh, yeah?

Mr Vaughan   That statue has stood in our beautiful school grounds,
undisturbed and in pristine condition, for nearly two
centuries. However, some ruffians, reputed to be
from this House, have seen fit to demolish it.

*There are stifled giggles. Mr Vaughan bangs
the table.*

Mr Vaughan   This is serious! Possibly a matter for suspension!

Hugo   Oh, no.

Ben   Ssh.

Charlie   He knows. I bet he knows.

Ben   Shut up and stop being such wimps.

Prefect   (*prodding Ben in the back*) Shut it, Russell Mi,[1] or
you'll be on newspaper duty and cookhole all week.

---

[1] Short for 'minor'. As boys are known by their surnames this shows he's a
younger brother.

| **Mr Vaughan** | Churchill House has a fine reputation in this school and I will not have its good name sullied by a few tearaways who seek to vandalise our heritage. You boys have managed to do what two world wars and all their bombs have failed to do: namely the destruction of the Perkins statue. Such vandalism will not be tolerated! I will give the perpetrators of this deed until six o'clock this evening to come forward and confess. I shall be in the Science block as usual during the day, and in my study this evening. I expect an answer. Otherwise the whole of this house will be gated for the duration. That will be all. |

Everybody groans and looks around to see if they can spot who did it. Ben notices that Hugo is staring at him. He stares back with a threatening look. Mr Vaughan snaps his Housebook shut and the meeting breaks up. Charlie has fallen asleep. Hugo goes over to Ben and Charlie.

Ben	(*prodding Charlie to warn him about Mr Vaughan*) Watch it, King Kong's looking at us.
Hugo	(*to Ben*) So, what are you going to do about it?
Ben	Bog off, de la Haye.
Hugo	I'm not talking to you.
Ben	Well, I'm talking to you.
Hugo	Don't threaten me, Russell.
Charlie	Leave it, Ben.
Ben	No, Big Mouth here had better watch it or –
Hugo	Or what?
Charlie	Ssh, Froggy's coming over.

Mr Vaughan wanders over to the boys. He has his hands behind his back – always a bad sign.

| **Mr Vaughan** | Ah, the Terrible Trio, the Three Musketeers. And what have we been up to lately, eh? |
| **Ben** | Nothing, Sir. |

Mr Vaughan	'Nothing, Sir.' I don't believe that for one second.
Ben	It's true, Sir.
Mr Vaughan	You, Russell, wouldn't know the truth if it came up and hit you in the face. And what about you, de la Haye?
Hugo	Me, Sir?
Mr Vaughan	(*staring fixedly at him*) Yes, de la Haye. You, Sir.
Hugo	Ah . . . I . . . I'm not with them, Sir.
Mr Vaughan	Oh? It looks very much to me as though you are, boy.
Hugo	No, Sir, I was just going.
Mr Vaughan	And what have these two done that you are so keen not to be tainted by?
Hugo	(*hesitating*) Ah . . . ah . . .
Mr Vaughan	Speak up, boy!
Hugo	Nothing, Sir.
Mr Vaughan	Don't you all play football together?
Hugo	(*panicking*) Look, Sir, it was nothing to do with me. I wasn't the one . . .
Mr Vaughan	The 'one' what, boy?
Ben	De la Haye, you turd!
Mr Vaughan	Falling out among thieves are we now? You may go, de la Haye.
	Hugo rushes off.
Mr Vaughan	I think I've found my culprits.
Ben	*What!*
Mr Vaughan	There. Didn't take long, did it?
Ben	I'll do him for that.
Charlie	Ssh, you'll just get us into more trouble.
Mr Vaughan	Right, you two boys, to my study. Now! Stand outside the door and wait until I come. Move an inch and that'll be the last moving you'll do for some days.

Charlie	Yes, Sir.

Mr Vaughan moves off.

Ben	He's a right sadist. I hate him. (*he looks at Charlie*) You all right, Charlie? You've gone all pale. You're not scared of Froggy, are you?
Charlie	No, just feel a bit tired, that's all.
Ben	Yeah, you dropped off during old Froggy's lecture. Didn't you sleep last night or something?
Charlie	I'm fine. Don't fuss.

Scene Three

Characters: Ben, Charlie, Hugo, Femi, Robert.

The Junior Common Room later that day. Ben and Charlie walk in. Everyone is immediately interested and mills round them.

Robert	What happened?
Femi	Are you being gated?
Robert	Or suspended?
Hugo	Bet you've been expelled?
Ben	Don't be a prat. Of course not.
Robert	What then? Come on, tell us.
Ben	It was the usual thing. He ranted and raved.

Ben imitates Mr Vaughan. He struts around shouting and everyone starts laughing. Charlie is the only one who doesn't. He sits down in a battered old armchair.

Charlie	Shut up, Ben, it's not funny.
Hugo	What's the matter with you, chicken or something? (*he clucks*) He looks like one, anyway.

Ben   Leave off, de la Haye.

Femi   You all right, Charlie?

Charlie   Yeah, leave me alone.

Femi   Only you look a bit pale.

Hugo   I told you, he's scared. Just trying it on so he can get out of Froggy's punishment.

Ben   Keep out of this, de la Haye. It's your fault we're in this mess. Grass!

Hugo   Oh, yeah, and what are you going to do about it?

They square up to each other. Robert stands between them.

Robert   Come on, Ben, he's not worth it. You're in enough trouble as it is.

Ben   Get him to keep out of my way or he'll be ending up in hospital.

Hugo   Oh, yeah? You and whose army?

Robert and Femi steer Ben away. Hugo makes gestures but only behind Ben's back, then he leaves.

Ben   He'd better watch it.

Robert   Just ignore him.

Femi   Tell us what old Froggy said.

Ben   Nothing much really. We're on Report. Big deal. And we've got to pay for the statue to be mended. That's all right. Charlie's old man's loaded. He can just ask him for some more pocket money.

Robert   Is that all? So why's Charlie looking as though they're going to send him home?

Ben   Don't know but you know what he's like; he worries about everything, and I bet he's a worried about what his mum's going to say.

Robert   Yeah, you should have seen her on Sports Day. Spent all her time going on at him. Nag, nag, nag.

Ben   Did you see that bloke she was with? Right div.

Femi His motor was all right, though, wasn't it? Red Ferrari. Yeah! Thundered through the school gates and nearly crashed into Soppy's pathetic old heap. I saw him come running out of the house throwing his arms about. It was a right laugh. And then Charlie's mum gets out of the car wearing that skirt. I nearly fell out of the window trying to get a better look at her and then the Head falls all over her being nice. I mean, it was sick.

Robert Did you see her in that film on telly over Christmas?

Ben No, but my dad and mum watched it. Dad thinks she's great and mum hates her.

Robert That's only because she's jealous.

Ben I know. My mum always wears these really boring old clothes and looks about 50.

Femi That's because she is 50.

Ben I wish she was like Charlie's mum.

Robert Bet your dad does too!

Charlie gets up unsteadily. He puts a handkerchief to his face.

Femi You OK, Charlie?

Charlie Yeah, just leave me alone, will you.

Femi All right. Only asking. Hey, your nose is bleeding!

Ben You'd better get to the bogs before you ruin old Froggy's carpet.

Charlie doesn't answer. As he walks away they notice he's limping slightly.

Femi Has he hurt himself playing rugger?

Ben He might have. He's been limping around for ages.

Femi There's definitely something wrong with him.

Ben Right, I'll go after him to see if he's all right.

Femi   OK, I'll catch up with you later. There's a
           programme I want to see on the telly.

           *He turns to the other boys watching TV, which is
           located in the Junior Common Room.*

Femi   Oi, you lot, out the way! I want to see this.

           *Ben runs off after Charlie and catches him up in the
           corridor. Charlie is resting against a notice board
           with his eyes closed. His nose is still bleeding.*

Ben   Hey, Charlie, you all right?

Charlie (*opening his eyes and straightening up*) Yes,
             I'm fine.

Ben   Only –

Charlie I said I'm OK! Right? How many times have I got to
             say it? Get lost, will you. (*pause as he looks at Ben*)
             Look, sorry, Ben, this stupid nose bleed won't stop
             and I'm feeling really whacked, that's all. I feel so
             tired I'm going to bed.

Ben   But it's only half-past eight.

Charlie So?

Ben   What's wrong with your leg?

Charlie Nothing.

Ben   But you're limping.

Charlie So? It's been like that for weeks.

Ben   So you should go to the San[1] and see the nurse
           about it. If you go first thing tomorrow you'll miss
           Froggy's Physics lesson.

Charlie Yes, that sounds neat.

Ben   I'll come with you. If you limp a bit more I can help
           you over there and I won't have to do Physics either.

           Charlie laughs and they walk off.

---

[1] Short for sanatorium, the room in a boarding school where sick people are treated.

Scene Four

*Characters: Charlie, School Nurse, Ben, Femi,
Robert, Hugo.*

*Charlie is in the San. The nurse runs it but a doctor
holds a regular surgery there for all the pupils.
Charlie is in a small room in an old-fashioned
hospital bed, which is very bouncy and creaky. He is
bored and keeps throwing a small rubber ball
against the opposite wall. The school nurse enters
and is nearly hit by the ball.*

School Nurse   Charles Massingham!

Charlie   Sorry.

School Nurse   The doctor's coming in to see you this morning.
(*handing him some medicine*) Drink this up, there's
a good boy. It's nothing too nasty. Just something to
keep your temperature down.

*Charlie takes the medicine from the nurse, but when
she turns away to look at his chart he pours it into
the glass of Coke on his bedside cabinet. When she
turns round he puts the medicine pot to his lips,
pretends to swallow and makes a face as though he
doesn't like the taste.*

School Nurse   Well done.

There is a lot of noise outside in the corridor.

School Nurse   What on earth?

*There are several loud knocks on the door and
when it opens Ben, Femi, Robert and Hugo enter.*

School Nurse   Boys, what are you doing here?

Hugo   Frog – I mean Mr Vaughan – said we could,
Nurse Towers.

School Nurse   (*looking at him suspiciously and then smiling*) Oh,
all right. Five minutes then and only five minutes.

Hugo   Yes, Nurse. Thanks.

She goes.

Femi   How you doing, man?

Charlie   Terrible. It's so boring in here. Hey, did old Froggy really say you could come?

Ben   No, but it's break-time and no one will miss us.

Robert   What you in here for then?

Charlie   Don't know. When Ben and me came in this morning she took one look at me and ordered me into bed. The doctor's seeing me later.

Femi   What does she think's wrong?

Charlie   I don't know. I've probably got a virus or something. Who cares? (*to Hugo*) Do you want this Coke?

Hugo   OK.

Charlie hands him the Coke with the medicine in it. Hugo drinks some and then spits it out.

Hugo   Ugh! What is it?

Charlie   I put my medicine in it.

Hugo   I'll get you for this.

He thumps Charlie on the leg.

Charlie   Ow! That hurt.

Hugo   What a little tap like that?

Charlie   It wasn't a little tap and, yes, it hurt. I'll probably have a bruise now.

Hugo   Not for that, surely.

Charlie   Yes, I've got loads of bruises. Nurse thought you'd all been beating me up!

Hugo   Hope you didn't tell her we have.

Charlie   No, seriously, I feel really achy all over.

Hugo   Flu. I'm getting out of here.

Ben   Don't be stupid

Hugo   What, then?

Ben	I don't know. I'm not the doctor. But he hasn't got flu.
Robert	(*bouncing on the bed*) Brilliant bed!
Charlie	Get off, you crummy toad, you're making me feel sick.
Robert	You missed a really good film on the telly last night. '*The Shallow Grave.*' It was great. Really cool. All those bodies. It scared the life out of me.
Femi	You'd better get back tonight. The semi-final of the Cup tie's on.
Charlie	Did United win last night?
Ben	Nah, lost two-nil.
Charlie	What, to *Brighton?*
Ben	Yeah. And Liverpool won.
Charlie	Oh, no. How many points are we down now?
Ben	Six, I think.
Charlie	(*groaning*) Typical.
Hugo	Do you still fancy that girl in Miss Heywood's form? What's her name? Catherine?
Charlie	What if I do?
Hugo	Nothing, just asking. Do you want to get off with her?
Charlie	Don't know. I sent her a letter through Greenwood's sister but she hasn't replied.
Hugo	Greenwood said she fancied you.
Robert	Watch him, he might be making it up.
Hugo	What, just to make you look a right Charlie.
Charlie	Oh, very droll.
Robert	Nah, he fancies her himself, don't you, de la Haye?
Hugo	Just shut up, will you?
Ben	We'll see her in Current Affairs this afternoon. Do you want us to ask her if she got your letter?

Charlie	No, I'll wait.
Hugo	Tell you what. We'll kidnap her and bring her round here after lights out.
Femi	You wish.
Ben	Keep out of this, de la Haye. You always muck things up.
Hugo	Yeah?
Ben	Yeah.

It looks like a fight again and they start to wrestle but the school nurse comes bustling in. Hugo and Ben move apart before the nurse notices anything.

School Nurse Right, boys, that's it. Time's up and anyway the bell is about to go for lessons.

Reluctantly they say good-bye and go.

School Nurse Now, young man, I've got to take your temperature and blood pressure and then you can rest. But first I need a tiny bit of blood. I won't hurt you, I promise.

Charlie (*disappearing under the covers fast*) Oh, no.

Scene Five

Characters: The Head Master Mr Appleyard, Mr Vaughan, Charlie's father Julian, Charlie, Charlie's mother Rachel, Paolo.

The Head Master, Mr Vaughan, Charlie and Julian are in the Head Master's study.

Mr A I'm glad you asked to see me, Mr Massingham. This business of the statue is very serious indeed. Though it's a little late in the day, if I may say so. It did happen some weeks ago.

Julian   Look, Appleyard, I'm not here for that pathetic
              statue. Just tell me how much it is and I'll sign a
              cheque straight away. It's more important than that,
              isn't it, son?

Charlie   Yes, dad.

Mr A   (*hesitant*) Where is your wife, by the way?

Julian   How on earth should I know? She said she was
              definitely coming.

Mr A   Oh, well, I'm sure she'll turn up soon.

Julian   With that boyfriend of hers in tow, no doubt.
              Anyway, I suggest we get on with it. I can't wait for
              her. I've got an important meeting this afternoon.
              The point is, Appleyard, that Charles is not well and
              the doctor is very concerned about him.

Mr A   Yes, we know he's had a spell in hospital.

Mr Vaughan And we know he hasn't been himself for some
              time, lacking concentration in class, always tired,
              and falling behind with his work. Would you say
              that was a fair assessment, Massingham?

Charlie   Yes, Sir.

Julian   Well, I'm not surprised because . . .

              *He is about to explain when they hear the throaty
              roar of a car as it approaches, screeches to a halt,
              and the doors slam shut. Laughter and voices are
              heard. There is a knock on the door and Rachel
              sweeps in followed by Paolo. Rachel is an actress in
              her late 30s, very glamorous but always putting on a
              performance. Paolo, an Italian footballer, is much
              younger than her.*

Julian   Oh, so you've managed to come then?

Rachel   Don't be so tiresome, Julian. My filming schedule
              is very tight. (*to Charlie*) Darling, how lovely to
              see you! You're looking so well. (*Julian groans*)
              Good afternoon, Mr Appleyard, and how are
              we today?

*Rachel does not like the Head Master who has only
been at Charlie's school for two terms; he is a weak
man and has let discipline slip. He is not at all like
the former Head Master whom the boys liked and
whose nickname was 'Old Thunderguts'. The boys
have no respect for the current Head Master and
call him 'Soppy'.*

Rachel   (*kissing Charlie and giving him a hug*) So what's my
sweet boy been up to?

Charlie   (*embarrassed*) Mum!

Paolo   Leave the boy, Rachel, can't you see he's
embarrassed.

Julian   If you'd looked after Charles properly when he
came to you –

Rachel   Don't you accuse *me* of not looking after him
properly. You never see him.

Julian   He's been with you the last two times and you
haven't even noticed he was ill.

Charlie   Dad!

Paolo   (*whispering to Charlie*) See the match on Saturday?

Charlie   Yeah, brilliant. Great goal you scored.

Paolo   Yes, not bad.

Rachel   (*getting dramatic and tearful*) Oh, my little baby!
He's got to go into hospital.

Julian   Why all the fuss now? You were supposed to be
looking after him and you didn't even notice he
was ill.

Rachel   Don't you talk to me like that. All you ever do is
spoil him.

Julian   At least I'm looking after him properly now. He's
going into a private hospital near me.

Rachel   I've got him booked into one near me.

Julian   Well, you can un-book him because he's going in
to mine.

Charlie	Mum. Dad.
Mr A	Dear me, parents, this is hardly the time or place.
Julian	Keep out of this, Appleyard, it's nothing to do with you.
Mr A	Please, for Charles' sake may we make some decisions about his schooling and so on.

Charlie suddenly gets up and rushes out. Both parents say together –

Rachel ⎫
Julian ⎬ There, now look what you've done.

Scene Six

Characters: Ben, Femi, Robert, Hugo, Charlie, Prefect, Mr Vaughan.

The Junior Common Room at 7pm some weeks later. The boys are supposed to be doing their prep but most of them are messing about and someone is playing pop music. Femi enters.

Prefect	Where've you been Adegboye?
Femi	The Washes.[1] Where else?
Prefect	A smoke, more like. Come on, get back to work.

Femi goes over to the others.

Femi	Guess what? Charlie's back.
Ben	What, now?
Femi	Yes, I've just seen his old man's Merc parked outside Soppy's house so he must be.

---

[1] Toilets and showers.

Ben Great.

Robert Yeah, it'll be great to have him back.

Mr Vaughan walks in and immediately the boys start scrambling about trying to look as though they are working.

Mr Vaughan Russell Mi, Chang, Adegboye, de la Haye!

All Yes, Sir.

Mr Vaughan Right, boys, listen. (*he addresses the entire room*) Turn that blasted music off!

The music stops and he turns back to the others.

Mr Vaughan Charles Massingham has returned to school this evening. As you know, he's been very ill and has been in hospital for many weeks receiving intensive treatment for leukaemia. But now he will be coming back with us during the week so that he can continue with school work and be in hospital at the weekends.

Femi Cor, that's not fair. No fun. He should be in hospital during school time.

Mr Vaughan From what I understand of what goes on in hospitals, Adegboye, I would say that it's far from dull.

Ben Can we visit him, Sir?

Mr Vaughan Anything to escape from here, eh? I'll try and make arrangements. Anyway, what I wanted to warn you about is that when you see Massingham for the first time you will notice . . .

He stops as he realises that all the boys are looking towards the Junior Common Room door. Charlie is standing in the doorway. He has lost weight and is bald. All eyes in the room have turned towards him. The boys gasp. One or two stifle giggles. Charlie stands there defiantly, challenging anyone to say anything. Ben breaks the spell first and moves towards him.

Ben   Charlie, it's great to see you back. All right?

Charlie   Yes, thanks.

Mr Vaughan   Ah, as you can see, Massingham is –

Hugo   Having a bad hair day, Sir!

Mr Vaughan   Well put as ever, de la Haye.

Robert   Charlie can't help it, Sir.

Mr Vaughan   Absolutely, Chang. It's good to see at least one of you has got some sense. Look, why don't you, Russell, and the others go off to the Common Room with Charles for a while. You can be excused prep for half an hour or so.

Ben   Thank you, Sir.

Hugo   Great.

Mr Vaughan   I'll leave you to it then.

He goes. Charlie's friends flock round him.

Femi   All right?

Charlie   All right.

Hugo   What happened? I mean, why . . . ?

Charlie   Why haven't I got any hair? It's the chemotherapy, the drugs they're giving me. It's one of the side-effects. There's nothing I can do.

Robert   Wear a wig.

Charlie   (*laughing*) Yeah, listen to this, right. There was this guy called Derek when I was in hospital, right, and last week he came to see me and . . .

They huddle together to listen. Lights crossfade to the ward.

Scene Seven

*Characters: Charlie, Derek Higginbotham, Louise
(a nurse).*

*Flashback to Charlie who is in hospital playing his
Game Boy as Derek enters. Derek is wearing a wig,
spectacles, a fairisle short-sleeved jumper, has a
very high-pitched voice, and carries a suitcase full of
exotic wigs and hats which he dumps on the table.*

Derek   Hello, you're Charles, aren't you?

Charlie   Charlie, actually.

Derek   Charlie, eh? OK, dear, you know why I'm here,
don't you?

Charlie   (*bored*) Yes, yes, you're going to show me some
wigs. Look, I told the nurses I don't want one.

Derek   Hold on a minute, dear. You might change your
mind when you see them.

Charlie   (*under his breath*) Doubt it.

Derek   (*completely over the top with enthusiasm*) Just look
at these, dear.

Charlie   (*to himself*) If he doesn't stop calling me 'dear', I'll
kill him.

Derek   Wonderful! The best! You, dear Charlie, can have
any wig you want.

Charlie   (*putting his Game Boy down*) Any? Seriously?

Derek   The truth or strike me down and hope to die.

*He makes a superstitious little gesture by crossing
his arms over his chest. Charlie is bemused.*

Charlie   What about a Mohican?

Derek   Two, if you want.

*Derek dives into his suitcase and brings out a
Mohican wig. Charlie immediately loses his bad*

*temper and tries it on. Derek holds up a mirror so
that Charlie can see himself.*

Charlie   Not bad. I'd like it in green and red, though.

Derek   Well, dear, if you choose it you can do what you
like with it.

Charlie   Got a purple one?

Derek   Purple, pink, mauve, mushroom, orange, oatmeal,
indigo, iris, barley, beige, cerise, sienna, terracotta,
taupe. (*he throws the wigs up in the air as he lists
them*) You, dearie, can have anything you want.

Charlie   All right, how about a clown's wig?

Derek   Yep.

Charlie   Pink punk?

Derek   Can do.

Charlie   Afro?

Derek   Curly as a wurly or dreadlocks, if you prefer.

Charlie   Is it just wigs you do?

Derek   No, I supply anything from black false teeth and
green moustaches to purple plastic noses. I mean,
there's no part of the extremities of the body that I
can't do. Listen, I've got this friend who supplies
prosthetics – that's the posh word for false legs to
you and me. Anyway, he fitted up this old boy with a
new false leg and the poor old geezer, who's a bit
lacking up top, is having trouble strapping the thing
on so my friend Kevin spends hours with him
practising how to keep the leg on. Anyway, comes
the day when the old boy's got to leave hospital and
all goes well until a couple of days later he goes to
get on a double decker bus. He puts his good leg up
on the deck and just as he's about to pull the false
one up it falls off. By this time the bus is ready to go
and drives off with this poor geezer's empty trouser
leg flapping in the breeze and his false leg lying in
the road!

Charlie is laughing.

Derek Ah, you can laugh, my dear, but it could happen to you. Supposing there's a high wind, or those naughty boys in your class snatch the wig off your bonce. What then, eh?

Charlie I don't think I'm going to wear one, Derek. I'll be like that swimmer, what's his name, Duncan Goodhew. Or I'll wear a hat.

Derek Now, there I can help you, dear. I have the most gorgeous hats you have ever seen.

Charlie Such as?

Derek Deerstalkers, cowboys, clowns, jesters, jockeys, beanies, bowlers, berets, trilbys, ten gallons, chefs, sheriffs, sou'westers, caps, top hats, Homburgs, helmets, pork pies –

Charlie All right, all right, I believe you.

Derek So what do you fancy, then?

Charlie A jester's hat.

Derek Here, what's your posh school going to say about that?

Charlie Old Froggy'll go ballistic.

Derek *Froggy?*

Charlie My House Master, Mr Vaughan. We call him Froggy.

Derek That's a bit naughty. What you going to call me then?

Charlie I can think of a few things for Higginbotham but I'm not going to tell you.

Derek Cheeky!

Louise, a young nurse, enters.

Louise Oh, it's you, Derek, I might have known. What are you up to? Charlie's supposed to be resting.

Derek (*indignant*) I'm doing my job, Nurse. I was told to come and see this young man about a wig and that's what I'm doing.

Louise   Well, I don't see much evidence of it.

Charlie   We're having a great time.

Louise   I can see that but you're meant to be resting.

Charlie   Not all the time.

Louise   No, but most of the time and that time's now.

She stands with her hands on her hips looking pointedly at Derek who grumbles as he starts to pack up his case.

Charlie   Aw, Louise, don't be a spoilsport!

Louise   You have to rest.

Charlie   Let him stay for a bit longer, please.

Louise   I can't, Charlie, I'm sorry. I'll have Sister after me.

Derek   She doesn't like me. She thinks I upset the patients.

Louise   You do.

Charlie   He doesn't. He's great!

Derek   Thank you, dear, it's nice to know someone appreciates me.

Louise   Come on, Derek, out.

Derek starts to leave.

Charlie   What about my Mohican and my jester's hat?

Derek   Another time. I have to go now. (*he nods his head at Louise and purses his lips*) Or Miss High-and-Mighty here will lose me my job.

Louise   Out. He's got to have some treatment.

Derek   All right, all right, I've got the message. Bye, dear, see you later.

Louise   Not today, Derek, his schedule's too busy.

Derek makes a tutting noise at her and flounces out. Charlie is angry and resentful that his fun has been stopped.

Charlie   Thanks a bunch, Louise!

Louise   It's no good being like that. You can't have your routine disturbed by Derek.

Charlie	But you told him to come.
Louise	We didn't tell him to mess about and tire you out.
Charlie	I'm not tired!
Louise	Well, it's time for your medicine.
Charlie	Ugh, not that stuff again.

They hear a crash offstage and Derek's and somebody else's protests. He has collided with a trolley and his case has burst open. The dialogue can be improvised offstage. Charlie bursts out laughing. Cut lights and bring up spot on the boys as at the end of Scene Six who are laughing at what Charlie has just 'told' them. Lights fade.

Scene Eight

Characters: Charlie, Ben.

The night following Charlie's return to school. It is dark and the others are asleep. Charlie is in his dressing gown and is standing outside the dormitory very upset and in tears. Ben appears. He is also in his dressing gown.

Ben	(*whispering*) Charlie? Charlie, is that you?
Charlie	Yes, over here.
Ben	You all right?
Charlie	(*turning away*) Yes.
Ben	It's OK, I know you're . . .
Charlie	Oh, man.
Ben	It's all right, I won't tell anyone. Listen, the others are all asleep. Do you want to get out of here?

Charlie Yeah.

Ben OK, what about the Norman Tower?

Charlie We can't. It's out of bounds. We'll be gated.

Ben Nobody'll know. Everybody's asleep, even old Froggy at this time of night. Come on. (*Charlie hesitates*) Look, if anything happens Robert or Femi'll cover for us.

Charlie OK, but what about de la Haye?

Ben He won't grass these days. Can you manage it as far as the Tower?

Charlie Yes, but I'll need some drink. My mouth gets so dry.

Ben We'll fill up a bottle of water from the cookhole.

Charlie OK.

They go. The lights dim then come up again on a moonlit country scene at the Norman Tower. Charlie and Ben, no longer in dressing gowns, enter and sit down against a tree.

Charlie I'm knackered!

Ben Well, you can rest here for a bit. We don't need to go back yet. Suppose you shouldn't have had that fag.

Charlie No, it was great. They all keep on about it, I'm not even supposed to be near smoke but I don't care. They can't take everything away from me.

Charlie starts coughing and can't stop.

Ben Here, have a drink.

Ben offers him the water bottle. Charlie drinks gratefully between coughs.

Ben How you feeling now?

Charlie Better, thanks.

Ben Uh, Charlie . . . was it anything really bad – back at the dorm, I mean?

Charlie Not really. It was just the thought of having to go back in again tomorrow. It's going to go on like this for months. I can't stand it, Ben. Apart from the treatment, which is just the pits, it's so boring. They treat you like a little kid and there's pathetic cartoon characters all over the walls and screaming babies and nurses who think you're a two-year old. I never thought I'd like school but it's great up to this. I tell you, I'm not going back!

Ben   Hey, man, you can't do that. You've got to finish your treatment.

Charlie   Yeah, that's what Frances keeps telling me.

Ben   Who's this Frances?

Charlie   Girl on our ward. She's got spina bifida and she's in a wheelchair but she's all right, you know. But look at me, Ben. I'm a right mess. No hair, and I've lost so much weight I'm a skeleton. I look like a geek. I used to play rugger and hockey, I used to fence and go cross-country running. Now I'm puffed out just walking to the Tower. What's the point in going on?

Ben   You're going to get better, that's what.

Charlie   Oh, yeah? When?

Ben   I don't know, but I bet it's not long now.

Charlie   It's all right for you. You don't have to have this treatment every day and you look normal. I'm a freak. Look at me! No girl's going to come near me looking like this.

Ben   You won't look like that forever though, will you?

Charlie   Who knows? All I know is I don't need all this, hospital and everything. Right?

Ben   Listen, it's not for ever, right, and we'll come and visit you. We asked old Froggy and he didn't say no. And we'll bring in some posters and we'll try to get Catherine and her friends to come in. Wa-hey!

Charlie   Don't let de la Haye come in. I hate him. And keep him away from Catherine.

Ben   OK. When do you have to go back in?

Charlie	Dad's picking me up at seven after supper on Sunday evening.

He puts his head in his hands to hide his face as he tries not to break down in tears.

Ben   Charlie, it's going to be all right.

Charlie (*his voice is breaking*) Who says?

Ben   You have to carry on.

Charlie (*angry*) It's all right for you! You don't have to have that disgusting chemo all the time. You don't have to drink litres and litres of water and then go to the loo in a urine bottle so they can measure it, or into a bowl for testing. It's gross. And I hurt all over. And the drugs and stuff they give you smell foul and it's always lurid colours like pink or mustard or yellow. Looks like sick and it makes you sick to drink it.

Ben   It'll be worth it in the end, won't it?

Charlie Who cares?

Ben   You are going to be all right, aren't you, Charlie?

Charlie (*looking away*) I don't know. I could die, Ben. They keep trying to hide it from me but I'm not a little kid, and I'm not stupid either.

Ben   (*fearful*) Did they tell you that?

Charlie No, but I know it anyway.

Ben   Have you thought about it? What it's like, I mean.

Charlie No, and I don't want to think about it.

Ben   Are you scared?

Charlie Yeah, really scared. Every time I go back in I think, is this it? Am I going to come out again?

Ben   (*upset*) Oh, man. (*pause*) What would I do without you, Charlie?

Charlie You'll find somebody else to be your best mate. Hugo.

Ben   No . . . no, I won't . . . especially not him. (*his voice is breaking*) Nobody's like you, Charlie.

Charlie   Yeah, well, tough.

Ben   Don't say that! You've got to hang in there, Charlie. Don't give in.

Charlie   I know what it was like for Joshua Perkins. I mean why his family had that statue.

Ben   I don't want some crummy statue of you.

Charlie   (*bitterly*) Yeah, well. (*pause*) They're talking about giving me a blood transfusion next time I go in.

Ben   Why? Have you been bleeding again?

Charlie   Not through a cut or anything, but they want to give me some more blood – 'platelets' they call them.

Ben   It sounds gross.

Charlie   (*desperately*) It's such a drag. I can't stand it any more, Ben, I can't.

He goes quiet and stares ahead. Ben doesn't speak for a while.

Ben   Have you talked to your mum or dad about this?

Charlie   No, they're too busy having a go at each other. I don't want to discuss it with them anyway.

Ben   Who do you want to go to when you get out of hospital?

Charlie   I don't care. They're both as bad as each other. It's pathetic. You're lucky, Ben, your parents are really great.

Ben   You should have to live with them. Dad's a workaholic and he thinks that just because he works hard all the time everybody else should too. He's always getting on at me and my brother about being lazy, and telling us how poor he was when he was little and how privileged we are and all that rubbish, and mum thinks we shouldn't swear or play our music loud and we should all wear nice clothes. She hates my heavy metal t-shirts and the music I play on my stereo. She doesn't know anything about music or sport, especially rugby.

Bet she thinks you play it with a hockey stick, and she keeps on at me all the time about the posters in my room but there's nothing wrong with them. They're great. Oh, and they expect me to go to church all the time. I mean, it's dead boring.

Charlie Yeah, I know what you mean. I'm going to leave home as soon as I can and do exactly what I like.

Ben Me too.

Charlie You know what I'd like now?

Ben No, what?

Charlie A McDonald's. Big Mac with large fries, a large Coke, and a hot apple pie.

Ben Don't, you're making my mouth water.

Charlie And after that, do you know what I'd like?

Ben What?

Charlie A Big Mac, with large fries, a large Coke –

Ben – and a hot apple pie.

Charlie Yeah!

Ben laughs and they drift off into their own thoughts for a moment.

Ben Look at that moon. It's fantastic to think people have actually been up there and walked on it.

Charlie One giant step for mankind. Wouldn't mind doing that myself.

Ben What, you want to go to the moon?

Charlie Yeah, wouldn't mind. I'd quite like to be an astronaut.

Ben I'd be scared to death.

Charlie Why?

Ben Well, I don't know really. I mean, you go right away from the earth. What if something happened?

Charlie It has, lots of times but they always manage to sort it out. It's better than flying and I reckon much safer.

Ben   Do you think we'll be living on other planets soon?

Charlie   Don't know. I think it's possible but not in our lifetime. (*pause*) You know, it's weird. I look up at the sky and the stars and there are thousands and thousands of them just in our galaxy alone. And there are loads of other galaxies out there and I think about myself fitting into all that. Just one person, one small lifetime and it feels really odd, like up against infinity and all that stuff. It's really mega and we think we're the only ones in the world, we think we're so clever on our planet.

Ben   That's because we are.

Charlie   Yeah, but who knows what else is out there? Much more advanced people than us, maybe.

Ben   Do you believe in all that stuff, aliens and all that?

Charlie   Why not? Frances believes in it. She believes in UFOs.

Ben   Well, I don't believe in them. I mean, it's just people off their heads seeing things.

Charlie   You wait. You might see something yourself.

They look up at the moon again. Suddenly Ben sits up.

Charlie   What's up?

Ben   Ssh. Up there. Look.

Charlie   Where?

Ben   Just by to the right of the moon in the sky. Look.

Charlie   I can't see anything.

Ben   It's all shiny and moving fast.

Charlie   Where?

Ben   Up there. Yeeow!

Charlie   (*getting desperate*) Ben, what is it? Tell me.

Ben   Little green men with two heads and four eyes!

Charlie realises he's been had and thumps Ben. They wrestle but not too seriously. Then they sit back and Charlie sighs.

Ben   You've got to hang on in there, Charlie. It'll be all right.

Charlie Yeah, well that's what Frances and everybody keeps telling me.

Ben   So you've got to believe it.

Charlie I don't know if I can.

Ben   You must. You have to. I don't know how I'd cope without you.

Charlie I know.

Ben   It's so unfair! Why did it have to happen to you?

Charlie Dunno, but it has. Hey, come on, cheer up. It's supposed to be me who's ill.

Ben   Yeah, sorry. Do you want to go now?

Charlie Yep.

            They get up.

Ben   Tell you what, we'll have a party for you in the dorm tomorrow night.

Charlie What about old Froggy?

Ben   He won't hear, it's Saturday. He'll be down the pub. What about it then?

Charlie Sounds great.

Ben   Right, I'll tell the others.

Charlie Ben.

Ben   Yes.

Charlie Thanks, mate. No, really, I mean it.

Ben   No sweat.

Scene Nine

Characters: Charlie, Ben, Femi, Robert, Hugo,
Catherine, Emily, Laura.

Saturday evening in the boys' dormitory. Catherine,
Emily and Laura are sitting together looking very
bored. Charlie is sitting opposite them. Robert
selects some music for the CD player.

Emily   Turn it down, Robert. We don't want to wake
Matron up!

Robert   No chance. Have you heard her snore? An
earthquake wouldn't wake her up. What do you
fancy next, Emily? (*the boys jeer at him*) I meant
music, you berks.

Emily   (*handing him a CD*) Heard this?

Robert   Oh, this is great! Where did you get it? I didn't think
you could get it over here.

Emily   You can't – yet. Dad bought it for me in America.

Hugo   Put it on, Robert.

Robert   OK. (*he does so and reads the CD cover*) This is
really cool. Was it their States tour?

Emily   Think so.

Hugo   They're releasing it here next month.

Laura   Bet it goes straight to the top. They're on tour soon.
Anybody coming to see them?

Robert   How can we if it's in term time?

Laura   Home weekend.

Robert   Oh, yeah, right. You get the tickets and we'll all
sleep over at your place. Your mum won't mind.

Laura   OK, you're on.

Robert   Great!

Femi walks in with a plateful of sandwiches.

Femi Sandwiches.

Catherine What's in them?

Femi Peanut butter and lemon curd.

Catherine What, all in together?

Femi Yes.

They all groan with disgust.

Femi What's wrong? They're cool.

Emily Disgusting, more like.

Laura Haven't you got anything else?

Femi Crisps, baked beans, canned sardines, and some jammy dodgers.

Laura Ugh!

Femi What do you want then?

Laura Haven't you got any yoghurt or fruit?

Femi What's that? Never heard of it.

Emily We don't want to eat that fattening junk.

Catherine I wouldn't mind some crisps.

Femi (*pouring some crisps into her lap*) Here you are then.

Catherine Femi! This is my best skirt. I only bought it last week.

Femi Sorry.

Catherine Well, get some tissues or something. If it's ruined you'll have to pay for it.

Femi Don't get so stressed, it's pretty naff anyway.

Catherine No, it's not. All the girls are wearing them.

Femi All girls must be daft then.

Emily (*indignant*) No, we're not.

While he looks for tissues, Catherine scoops up the crisps and dumps them in his bed under his duvet.

Robert Want to dance, Em?

Emily	No thanks.
Hugo	How about me then?
Emily	Yeah, all right.

They get up to dance and Hugo jeers in triumph at Robert who has a go at him in return. Femi comes back and sits next to Catherine and tries to brush off her skirt but she pushes him away.

Catherine	Get off me, Femi.
Hugo	Whey, that's what he's trying to do! He fancies you.
Femi	Talking about yourself, de la Haye?
Robert	Anyone want a drink?
Laura	What have you got?
Robert	Coke, lemonade, Five Alive –
Laura	How exciting can you get?
Robert	No, wait, and –
Laura	Yes?
Robert	Some cider.
Laura	I'm going. It's a dead loss in here (*to Catherine*) You coming?

They get up to go, but Femi stops them.

Femi	Look, don't go. We're here for Charlie, right? He's going back tomorrow and they'll be starting his treatment again.

Reluctantly, the girls sit down again. Catherine stares at Charlie as if she can't come to terms with his looks. Charlie becomes defensive.

Charlie	What?
Catherine	Nothing.
Charlie	Yes, there is. You look as though you're about to puke all over me. What are you staring at? Haven't you ever seen a bald person before?
Laura	She didn't mean anything, Charlie.
Charlie	No? Well why look at me like that then?

Laura   I told you.

Charlie   I know what she's thinking. (*to Catherine*) Why
               don't you say what you're thinking, eh? It's like
               being in a circus! Poor old Charlie, he's a right freak.
               (*he rolls up his sleeve*) Look, look. Do you want to
               see all my bruises and the needle marks too?

               Catherine is fighting back tears.

Laura   Leave her alone, Charlie! She didn't mean it.

Charlie   Yeah, well she shouldn't gawp at me then, should
               she? And when I come back next time I'll have grown
               two heads. Then you can really have something to
               puke over. To think I fancied you once!

Laura   That's horrible, Charlie.

Charlie   (*he points to his head*) Oh, yeah, and you think
               this isn't.

Laura   (*shouting*) That doesn't give you the right to act
               like a moron!

Charlie   (*shouting back*) It takes one to know one!

Catherine Stop it! Stop it, both of you.

               *Ben has entered with some pizzas in boxes and
               hears the shouting.*

Ben   What's going on?

Femi   Nothing.

Ben   Don't be stupid. Why are you all shouting at
               each other?

Hugo   Nothing to do with me.

Charlie   Ask her.

Catherine Ask him.

Ben   (*to Catherine*) Come over here a minute.

               *They go to a far corner and sit down where the
               others can't see them.*

Ben   This was meant to cheer Charlie up, not make him
               feel worse.

Catherine	I'm sorry, I really am. I didn't mean to hurt him. It's just that . . . honestly, Ben, it's ever so difficult not to stare at him but he looks so weird at the moment and then he sees you looking at him and he gets all upset. (*she is tearful again*) I used to really like him, Ben, but he's changed so much. He's really horrible now.
Ben	He can't help it, Catherine, it's the treatment.
Catherine	I know but –
Ben	It won't be for ever. You've got to help him, not get up his nose.
Hugo	(*coming up to them*) I think you should go and see to the pizzas. I'll look after Catherine.
Ben	(*getting up*) Thanks.
Hugo	So what's up then?
Catherine	Ben thinks I'm being horrible to Charlie but I can't help it. Oh, Hugo.
	Hugo gives her his handkerchief. Unknown to them Charlie is watching and listening.
Hugo	(*putting his arm round her*) Better now?
Catherine	Yes. I didn't mean to be horrible to him.
Hugo	I know, don't worry about it.
Catherine	He is going to be all right, isn't he?
Hugo	I don't know but everyone's hoping he will.
	They fall silent for a while.
Hugo	You all right now?
	She nods. He tries to kiss her. She pulls away.
Catherine	No!
Hugo	Why?
Catherine	Charlie –
Hugo	I know, but I thought you two didn't get on any more.
Catherine	We don't but I don't think I could do this to him, Hugo.
Hugo	Why? Because you feel sorry for him?

Catherine	Yes – I mean no – but aren't you supposed to be one of his best friends?
Hugo	He won't mind. Well, then?
Catherine	I don't know.
Hugo	I really fancy you – and I know you like me.
Catherine	Don't, Hugo, it's not fair.
Hugo	Oh, come on, he's not going to know. He's going back into hospital tomorrow. (*pause*) Please.
Catherine	Don't push me.

She looks away. Hugo puts his hand on her face and pulls her round to look at him. They stare at each other and Hugo looks as if he is going to kiss her when Charlie rushes past them out of the room swearing at him. Ben rushes after him.

Ben Hugo, you . . . Charlie! Charlie!

ACT TWO

Scene One

Characters: The Registrar Ms Haden, Sister, Julian, Rachel.

Ms Haden's office. They are all discussing Charlie's illness.

Ms Haden Your son's illness is very serious, I'm afraid.

Rachel Does that mean that he's . . . that . . .

Ms Haden That he's going to die? (*Rachel nods unhappily*) No, not necessarily. This type of leukaemia has a high rate of recovery although, of course, we cannot guarantee anything.

Julian Always have to cover yourselves, don't you?

Ms Haden It's not a question of covering ourselves, Mr Massingham. We have to be honest and realistic. You asked to see me because you wanted to be absolutely clear about Charles's illness and his chances of recovery. I am being as straight with you as I possibly can but you must understand that we cannot say at this stage exactly how he's going to be in the long term.

Julian Well, what *exactly* can you tell us?

Ms Haden At the moment Charles is responding well to his treatment. It's very unpleasant and painful, and as you know the side effects are not very nice. But he's putting up with it very well.

Rachel Putting up with it?

Ms Haden Yes, well what I meant was that some children find it very hard to be in hospital for long periods. It's

	very boring. Charles is an intelligent boy and he was very active at school, I believe?
Rachel	Yes, he played rugby and cricket and things like that. He was in all the teams.
Ms Haden	And now he feels tired all the time and has no energy to do anything, and this is particularly difficult for someone sporty like him.
Julian	Why can't we have him home then? He wouldn't be bored there.
Ms Haden	Because, Mr Massingham, Charles's treatment has to be monitored very carefully. We have to do tests all the time on the effect of the drugs we give him. He feels sick most of the time and very tired. Also, at some stage in his treatment he will have to be in complete isolation because we will not be able to risk him catching any infections of any kind. He has to be in hospital for that.
Rachel	Isn't being bald bad enough? My poor Charlie!
Ms Haden	There is also the possibility that he will need a bone marrow transplant.
Rachel	Oh!
Ms Haden	Don't worry, it's a fairly safe procedure these days but I'm afraid there's always the risk that this won't work, that the body will reject the new bone marrow but the good news is there's a new transplant treatment being developed which carries less risk of rejection and Charlie may benefit from that.
Julian	How long's all this going to go on for?
Ms Haden	Some months at least until he's in what we call remission. This means until all signs of the illness have gone and he seems better again.
Rachel	Don't you mean cured? Why do you call it remission?
Ms Haden	Because we can't guarantee that it won't come back again.
Rachel	(*becoming tearful*) Oh, no.

Julian He'll be all right, Rachel, you'll see. He's a fighter, our son, he'll come through.

Rachel But what if he doesn't, Julian, what then?

Julian Don't upset yourself. He will. We've got to think of Charles, not ourselves. So what's his chances, doctor?

Ms Haden Quite good. In three out of four cases, Mr Massingham, patients with this sort of leukaemia are cured. We can only hope that Charles is one of them.

Julian When will you know that?

Sister He will be on maintenance therapy for two or three years but this will be mostly outpatient treatment. We shall know better then.

Rachel Two or three *years?*

Julian That long?

Ms Haden In most cases, yes, so he will need a lot of support from home, from his friends and the school.

Julian and Rachel are very subdued by this and sit for a moment trying to take it in. Rachel sniffs and the registrar hands her some tissues.

Rachel What if . . . what if he isn't . . . one of the lucky ones?

Ms Haden Well, we do have patients who die but, as I said before, most of them don't and we have to hope that Charles isn't one of those who do. Whatever happens you will get lots of support from us and we'll keep you informed all the way through. The important thing is to make sure that Charles believes he's going to get better not only because that helps him to cope with the difficult treatment but also because a positive attitude really does help patients to get better. Any more questions? (*Julian and Rachel both shake their heads*) Right, well if you'll excuse me I must get on. (*she gets up and shakes hands with Charlie's parents*) Nice to have met you both and don't hesitate to see us again if you have any further questions at any time.

*Ms Haden goes out. Julian and Rachel stand up
ready to leave.*

Julian   I need a drink after this. You coming?

Rachel   Yes, I think I need one.

Julian   *(he smiles)* Good. Just like old times, eh?

Scene Two

*Characters: Charlie, Frances, Louise, Sister,
Dr O'Donnell (a Consultant), Ms Haden, Mr Singh
(House Doctor), Medical Students Miss Johnson,
Miss Kumani and Mr Young.*

*Charlie's hospital room. Frances is there in her
wheelchair. Derek has given him some silly hats
and wigs which he uses to entertain her and he is
wearing one of them now. They hear Dr O'Donnell's
booming voice offstage.*

Frances   That's the doctors. I'd better go.

Charlie   You can stay, Frances. I don't mind.

Frances   No, they won't let me. I'll see you later. Bye.

*She wheels herself out and the others come in.
When the doctors or nurses enter Charlie usually
does his best to annoy them. This morning is the
'royal' visit from the Consultant, Dr O'Donnell, who
wears a sharp suit and is very aware of his
importance. The others, except Sister, have white
lab coats on. Charlie is listening to his personal
stereo when they enter and crowd round his bed.*

Ms Haden   Charles Massingham, Dr O'Donnell. (*she hands him
the notes*) Acute lymphoblastic leukaemia.

O'Donnell	(*looking at the notes*) Mmm. Yes. . . Mm, I see. And how is he?
Charlie	(*shaking his head to the music*) OK so far, doctor, but don't mind me.
Ms Haden	Very well, so far.
O'Donnell	Well done, well done. And what is the prognosis,[1] Mr Singh?
Charlie	(*to himself*) Very good so far, doctor, and responding well to treatment, as you can see.
Mr Singh	Very good so far and he's responding well to treatment, as you can see.
O'Donnell	(*looking at Charlie and his stereo*) Yes, quite. And what are we giving him?
Charlie	This drug, that drug, the other drug. All disgusting.
O'Donnell	And what, Mr Young, is special about these drugs?
Charlie	Cytotoxic.
Mr Young	(*glancing at Charlie, amazed*) They are cytotoxic drugs, Sir.
O'Donnell	Yes, coming from the Greek. Meaning what, Miss Kumani?
Miss Kumani	Highly poisonous.
O'Donnell	No, no, what do the Greek words mean?
Miss Kumani	I don't know, Dr O'Donnell.
O'Donnell	What sort of education are they giving you people these days? (*Charlie mouths the answer as he says it*) 'Cyto' meaning hollow vessel and 'toxic' meaning poisonous. Yes, highly poisonous which is why we have to regulate them so carefully. Isn't that so, Sister?
Sister	Yes, Dr O'Donnell.
O'Donnell	However, we aim to poison the disease not the patient!

---

[1] What will happen to the patient.

*He laughs loudly at his own joke. Charlie yells out a
line of the music and makes everyone jump.*

O'Donnell   Nasty but highly effective – and I'm not talking
about this young man's singing. (*they all laugh on
cue*) Right, let's have a look at his chest, Miss
Johnson.

*The medical student nervously fumbles for the
stethoscope in her coat pocket which she drags out
and drops on the floor. After retrieving it she goes
to Charlie.*

Miss Johnson   Could you sit up a bit, please?

Charlie   (*deliberately not hearing*) What?

Miss Johnson   Sit up, please.

Charlie   Sorry, can't hear.

Sister   Charles, take those things out of your ears.

*She waits as Charlie slowly removes them and then
she puts them to one side.*

Sister   And sit up!

Charlie   Hey, they're mine. That's stealing.

O'Donnell   (*sternly*) Young man . . .

*Charlie makes a face and sits forward reluctantly
with a great fuss. Miss Johnson puts her stethoscope
on his back to listen to his lungs.*

Charlie   (*pushing her stethoscope away*) Hey, that's cold!

Sister   (*warning*) Charles.

Miss Johnson   Sorry.

*She moves the stethoscope to his chest as Charlie
takes deep rasping breaths.*

Miss Johnson   Could you breathe normally, please?

Charlie   No, your hands are freezing. You're making me
all cold.

Sister   Now, Charles, that's enough, the doctor's doing her
best. Try to co-operate.

Charlie I feel sick.

Sister The sick bowl's right beside you.

Charlie I need a pee.

Sister (*becoming impatient*) I'll get a nurse to help you in a minute.

O'Donnell Well, Miss Johnson, what can you hear?

Miss Johnson Pop music mostly, Dr O'Donnell.

Everyone except Dr O'Donnell laughs. He frowns.

O'Donnell And how would you say he is feeling, Sister?

Charlie Like a prize animal in a zoo.

Sister Rather bored, I fear.

O'Donnell Good, good. Well, keep up the good work. Onwards.

Charlie (*mimicking him*) Keep up the good work. Onwards.

Dr O'Donnell sweeps out followed closely by everybody except Mr Young.

Mr Young What you listening to?

Charlie Slaughter.

Mr Young Let's have a listen. Haven't heard this lot since my student days.

Charlie offers him an earphone, which he puts it to his ear. Together they sing along, making a terrible noise.

Mr Young Ugh, did I really like this? Sounds like somebody trying to vomit!

Charlie It's great.

Mr Young (*pointing to the vomit bowl, shaped like an upside down bowler hat*) I should keep that bowler hat beside you, if I were you.

He makes vomit noises and Charlie laughs.

O'Donnell (*bellowing offstage*) Young!!

Mr Young Oops, got to go. The Tyrant King summons. See you, mate. Stay cool. Keep listening.

Charlie   Yeah, see you.

He goes. Charlie lies back and looks bored. Louise enters carrying a urine bottle.

Louise   Sister said you needed this.

Charlie   No.

Louise   Charlie!

She goes out. Charlie waits a few moments then he presses the buzzer. A light flashes above his bed. He waits and then Louise enters without the bottle and switches off the buzzer light. Charlie smiles.

Charlie   Mmm, nice perfume.

Louise   (*ignoring his remark*) Well?

Charlie   Well what?

Louise   What do you want?

Charlie   I think I need the bottle now.

Louise   Charlie, I've got better things to do than run around after you. We're very busy today. We had two emergency admissions in the night.

Charlie   Sorree. Can't help it.

Louise   If it wasn't for the fact that you have to stay in here I'd make you use the toilets on the main ward.

Charlie   Well, if they gave me a room with a bathroom, instead of this crummy one, I'd wouldn't have to keep asking you.

Louise   You'll want a five-star hotel next.

Charlie   Yeah, with lots of maids in short skirts!

Louise   You are getting cheeky.

Charlie   You still fancy that doctor?

Louise   It's none of your business.

Charlie   Haven't you got off with him yet? I'll ask him to fix a date with you, if you like.

Louise   You just dare.

Charlie Don't think he's much of it, myself. Like, he fancies himself too much. You'd be better off with old thingummy, you know with Mr Funface, um . . . Dr Young. He's cool. I'll tell him you want to go out with him.

Louise Don't you dare! Oh, and while I think of it, what did you put in your last urine sample?

Charlie What?

Louise You know what I'm talking about. We couldn't do a proper test because you'd put something in it. What was it? Sprite, lemonade?

Charlie (*laughing*) Didn't the lab analyse it and tell you?

Louise No, they did not. They've better things to do with their time and money. I want a proper sample next time. No adulterations. (*losing her patience*) Do you want to spend a penny or not?

Charlie Nah, changed my mind.

Louise Well, if you call me in again for nothing I'll tell Sister.

Charlie (*pretending to be worried*) Ooh no, don't do that, Louise, please, Louise.

She shakes her head at him and goes. Charlie laughs then lies back and closes his eyes, smiling.

Scene Three

Characters: Charlie, Frances, Louise, Vera (a Staff Nurse).

Some weeks later. There is a timid knock at the door. Charlie lies back in bed and closes his eyes. Frances enters in her wheelchair.

Frances Charlie, are you awake?

Charlie Yeah, just pretending in case the nurses come in. It's time for my treatment. What are you doing in here?

Frances Visiting. I know I'm not meant to but –

Charlie You can't survive without seeing me.

Frances (*embarrassed*) Charlie. I just thought I'd –

Charlie I know, only teasing. How you feeling?

Frances (*struggling for a moment to find a voice*) They want to operate again.

Charlie *Again?* But that makes six you'll have had.

Frances I know. I don't want any more operations, Charlie, I've had enough!

Charlie Look, Frances, I know how you feel. I mean I'd feel the same right but, like, sometimes we just have to do what they say for our own good. Right? It'll be OK in the long run, you'll see.

Frances I just want to go home.

Charlie Yeah, don't we all.

Frances If it wasn't for this stupid wheelchair I'd walk out of here and never come back.

Charlie Great. We can run away together.

Frances I didn't say I wanted you to come with me.

Charlie Oh, thanks.

Frances   I didn't mean it like that but it's just, you know, I want a bit of time on my own. You never get any peace in this place.

Charlie   I know. I mean, those rotten little babies screaming their heads off all the time. They should just stuff them in their cots and give them a shot of something to shut them up. I would.

Frances   That's really mean. They're only babies. (*she sighs*) Oh, there's this really sweet one with ginger hair. (*Charlie groans*) And he's got such a lovely smile. I keep wanting to cuddle him.

Charlie   I shouldn't. He'll be sick, or pee all over you. Or worse.

Frances   That's horrible. They can't help being ill.

Charlie   Well, they should be ill somewhere else. Not near me.

Frances   You're a right misery today. What's the matter?

Charlie   Nothing.

Frances   Charlie.

Charlie   What?

Frances   What's the matter?

Charlie   Nothing. I'm fed up, that's all.

Frances   Join the club. If I have this op, I won't be able to play my violin for ages.

Charlie   Is that bad then?

Frances   Of course it is! It's the only thing I can really do well. Look at me! I'm all twisted, I can't walk, I can hardly do anything for myself without having help but it's different with my violin. I can play it without anybody having to help me, when I want, on my own.

Charlie   So how long will it take before you can play again?

Frances   I don't know. They won't really tell me. They keep fobbing me off.

Charlie   You will though, won't you? I mean, play again.

Frances   (*quietly*) I don't know, Charlie.

She puts her head on the bed and starts to cry.
Charlie reaches out to hold her hand as she
struggles to keep back the tears.

Charlie   It'll be OK, Frances, you'll see. Bet you'll be as good as what's-her-name, Jacqueline de Something – my mum likes her stuff. It's terrible.

Frances   Jacqueline du Pré and she's plays the cello, not the violin. Anyway, she's dead.

Charlie   Oh, sorry. I suppose you not being able to play again is a bit like my hair. I don't know if it's going to grow back or not.

Frances   It will. I've seen loads of people when they've finished their chemo and their hair always grows back again.

Charlie   Great. Bet you see loads of people come and go. It's like you live here.

Frances   I know. I reckon I've been in hospital more times than I've been home.

Charlie   (*suddenly shouting*) Aaghh! Was that Louise?

Frances   (*looking to see*) I think so. Why?

Charlie   Where can I hide?

Frances   Don't be such a wimp.

Charlie   Speak for yourself.

Louise enters. Charlie dives under the covers. Louise
stops when she sees Frances.

Louise   Frances! What are you doing in here? Charlie is not meant to have any visitors. We have to prevent any infection. You know that.

Frances   Yes, I'm sorry.

Louise   You could really jeopardise his chances of a bone marrow transplant by being here.

Frances   I'm really sorry. I said I'm sorry.

Louise	Well, that's not good enough. Come on, out.
	Frances starts to leave.
Charlie	(*emerging from under the covers*) Leave her alone, Louise. She only came in to say hello.
Louise	Well, she's not supposed to. You can't risk any cross-infection.
Charlie	Stop picking on her. (*pointedly*) Bye, Frances. See you later when Dragonface here isn't looking.
Louise	Charlie, that's enough.
	Frances goes out.
Louise	OK, let's get this over with.
Charlie	No!
Louise	Oh, not again, Charlie. Come on, I haven't got time for this.
Charlie	No, no, no!! Get off me, you dragon.
	Louise tries to get him co-operate but he fights her off. She presses the buzzer and the light goes on.
Louise	Charlie, this isn't doing you any good, you know it isn't. You've got to have this treatment.
Charlie	Naff off, you sadist.
	Vera appears. She is a staff nurse in her 50s and much older than Louise. She is firm but motherly.
Vera	Now, Charlie, what's all this?
Louise	He won't have this again, Staff.
Vera	Well, I know how you feel –
Charlie	No, you don't. How many times have you ever had to take this stuff?
Vera	That's not the point. Why don't you try to make it easy for Louise?
Charlie	Look at all these bruises.
Vera	That's not Louise's fault. We've got very few places left where there isn't some damage from the drugs. She's doing her best. Come on, Charlie.

Charlie   No, I'll feel sick.

Vera   Listen, I'll stay and hold your hand, OK?

Charlie   Big deal.

Vera   You'll only make it worse if you try to fight us.

Charlie   No!

Vera   (*coaxing gently*) Come on, sweetheart, a quick top up through this tube. You know it won't hurt.

Charlie   No, not now but I'll feel really manky later.

Vera   Come on.

Charlie   (*giving in*) OK, but only 'cos it's you.

Vera   (*holding his hand*) There's my darling. It won't take a second.

Charlie   (*to Louise*) Then you can get lost!

Louise   Don't worry, I'm going.

She administers the drugs through a tube and goes. Charlie is exhausted, angry and close to tears.

Vera   I know, I know, pet. Everything they do to you in here is so awful but one day, Charlie, you'll be better and you'll forget all this and you can go and live a perfectly normal life again.

Charlie   I'm not going to make it, Vera, I know I'm not. I don't want to go on with this any more, I can't take any more. What's the point in going on?

Vera   You feel like that at the moment, pet, but believe me when you're walking out of here all better you'll be glad you hung on.

Charlie   I can't. I can't.

Vera   Yes, you can. You've got to. You must.

Charlie buries his face in his pillow and Vera stays to comfort him.

Scene Four

Characters: Charlie, Rachel, Julian, Ben, Night Nurse, Sister.

It is night time in the hospital. Moonlight floods through the window creating an eerie glow in the room. The ward is quiet and Charlie is lying in his hospital bed very ill, surrounded by equipment which blips and hisses. Spotlights come up on his mother and father, one to the left and one to the right of him but they are not really there, they are only in Charlie's dream. Everybody speaks as though they are the only ones there. He does not look at his parents when they talk but stares straight ahead.

Julian   They've got it all under control, son. You'll be better soon, you'll see.

Charlie   Hi, Dad, how are you?

Julian   Don't worry, there's no chance we'll let you go.

Charlie   Yeah, I'm trying my best, Dad.

Julian   Your mother's here, too.

Charlie   Hi, Mum.

Rachel   It's taken me absolutely ages to get here. I had to cut a rehearsal and the Director was less than pleased, I can tell you, and the traffic was simply ghastly. But never mind, I'm here now.

Charlie   It's great to see you.

Rachel   Your father wants custody when you're better but I'm not very happy about it, I can tell you.

Charlie   I hate it in here. Do you know when I can go home?

Julian   Everyone's doing their best for you, son. Now it's up to you. But you're going to be all right, we know you are. You just have to fight it. Don't give in, OK?

Charlie	I've tried so hard.
Rachel	We know this must be really horrible for you, darling, but we're here for you.
Charlie	I'm really scared, Mum.
Julian	It's not nice, all this. We know that.
Charlie	I'm really scared, Dad.
Julian	They'll be letting you out soon, won't they? Look at you. You look fine.
Charlie	I keep thinking I'm going to die.
Rachel	You're looking so much better.
Charlie	I don't want to die.
Rachel	I'm not worried about you, Charlie, because I know you're going to be all right.
Charlie	(*desperate*) Mum!
Rachel	Must go, darling. I'm recording a voice-over for a new car ad.
Julian	You're doing all right, son. Hang on in there.
Charlie	(*desperate*) Dad!
Julian	You'll be fine, son, just don't think about it. (*his mobile phone rings and he answers it*) Hello . . . yes, Jimmy . . . OK . . . well, we'll have to go ahead then . . . yes, right, I'll be there. (*he rings off*) Bye, then, son. Got to go. Business.

They both go. Charlie rubs his eyes with the back of his hand. Ben appears by Charlie's side. Like Charlie's parents, he isn't really there.

Ben	Hi, Charlie, great to see you. All right?
Charlie	No, I'm very ill actually
Ben	Hey, look at that moon. Remember the moon at the Tower, Charlie?
Charlie	Yeah.
Ben	You said you wanted to be an astronaut.

Charlie And you said you'd be scared to death. I'm scared, Ben, but not about going to the moon.

Ben I know. It'll be all right though.

Charlie That's what everybody says. It's all right for them.

Ben You'll make it, Charlie. I know you will. We're all thinking about you. Hey, listen to this. Know that Gerard dude, that creep in Balmoral House, right? Well, he's only gone berserk in Chemistry and smashed a load of equipment.

Charlie What happened?

Ben He said everyone was getting at him. Bullying him all the time. He's a right div. It was really funny, yeah. Old Bunga Bear had to get him in this wrestling hold to stop him from doing any more damage. Right laugh. They were dancing round the lab and he was screaming and carrying on. Later on his mum had to come and take him home – or the loony bin, more like.

Charlie Yeah, I know how he feels. (*pause*) How's Catherine?

Ben (*feeling awkward*) Oh, OK.

Charlie Is Hugo still going out with her?

Ben Uh . . . yes. Look, Charlie –

Charlie It's all right. I fancied her once but not any more. I saw the way she looked at me.

Ben She didn't mean anything by it, Charlie.

Charlie No? Well, I heard what she said.

Ben Yeah, well she's really sorry about that but you've got to understand how difficult it is for everyone, you know, you being like this. They all feel really sorry for you.

Charlie I don't want their pity!

Ben (*changing the subject*) Do you fancy anyone in here?

Charlie	Yes . . . (*he hesitates*)
Ben	Don't tell me then, will you? Is it one of the nurses?
Charlie	No, don't be stupid. I mean, they wouldn't look at me, I'm just a kid to them. You know Frances? It's her.
Ben	But she's in . . . (*he stops*)
Charlie	Yes?
Ben	I mean . . .
Charlie	She's in a wheelchair and she's a cripple?
Ben	(*feeling very uncomfortable*) Like, I don't mean to be offensive or anything but she's not exactly . . . well, good looking or anything, is she?
Charlie	So what?
Ben	Well, nothing, I suppose, if you don't mind that sort of thing and you like her.
Charlie	I do.
Ben	That's all right then.
Charlie	She's really brave and she's really brilliant.
Ben	Yeah, OK.
Charlie	She plays the violin brilliantly.
Ben	Yeah, all right.
Charlie	I don't care if she isn't like some model or whatever.
Ben	No.

There is a pause, then Ben tries to break the awkwardness.

Ben	Seen any more little green men since the Tower?
Charlie	Shut up, man!

Ben makes faces and frightening noises and they laugh. Then Charlie sits up in bed and stares out at the moon. The night nurse enters and Ben goes.

Night Nurse	Charlie, what are you doing?
Charlie	I'm looking at the moon.

Night Nurse	What's up? Can't you sleep?
Charlie	No. It's beautiful, isn't it?
Night Nurse	Yes, lovely.
Charlie	I want to go there when I die.
Night Nurse	What?
Charlie	You know some people think that you go to heaven when you die? Well, I'm going to the moon, that's going to be my heaven.
Night Nurse	You're a deep one, Charlie, too deep for me. Come on, lie back. You'll get cold.
Charlie	Two more minutes.
Night Nurse	OK, but then lie down and try to get some sleep.

She goes. Charlie continues to stare at the moon. Then he lies back and closes his eyes. Lights crossfade to show time has passed. Sister enters with Rachel.

Sister	He's very ill, Mrs Massingham. He's asleep at the moment so it's best to sit quietly beside him until he wakes up.
Rachel	(*tearful*) Yes, Sister.

Sister goes and Rachel sits down at the bedside and holds Charlie's hand and whispers.

Rachel	Oh, Charlie, Charlie.

Julian enters. He stops when he sees Rachel. He waits a moment then he goes over and puts a hand on her shoulder.

Julian	It's all right, love, he'll be all right, you see.
Rachel	Look at him. He looks so pale. He looks –
Julian	No, he's going to be all right. We'll see him through, you'll see. Come on, son, don't give in. Fight! Fight it. We're here for you. It's mum and dad. We're both here.

His voice starts to break and Rachel turns to him and they hold each other.

Scene Five

Characters: Julian, Rachel, Sister.
Sister is talking to Charlie's parents.

Sister   Good news, Mr and Mrs Massingham. Charles is responding well to his treatment at last. I think we can say we're over the worst for the time being.

They both sigh with relief. Julian pats Rachel's arm and she smiles back at him.

Julian   Can we see him now?

Sister   Of course, there are no restrictions on visiting and he's not in isolation any more.

Rachel   Uh . . . I'm sorry . . . I can't stop at the moment. I'm recording a commercial this morning and then I'm meeting Paolo. I might be able to drop in this evening though.

Julian   And I thought you'd changed.

Rachel   I'm seeing him later and you're going in now, aren't you?

Julian   Somebody has to assume responsibility round here.

She goes.

Julian   Better go and see my boy.

As he gets up his mobile phone rings.

Julian   Yes, who's speaking?

Sister   Mr Massingham, you are not supposed to have those things switched on in here. They may interfere with equipment.

Julian   (*waving at her to be quiet*) I'll only be a minute . . . yes . . . OK . . . what, now? . . . oh, all right.

Ten minutes . . . yes, see you then. Bye. (*he switches off the phone*) Look, urgent business, I'm afraid. I'll pop in and see Charles later.

He goes. Sister is not impressed.

Scene Six

Characters: Charlie, Ben, Robert, Femi, Hugo, Frances, Louise, Vera.

Charlie's room some time later. He is much better and playing on his Game Boy. Vera enters.

Vera   Charles Massingham, I've got a bone to pick with you. I can tell you're over the worst.

He ignores her and eventually she puts her hand over his Game Boy.

Vera   Charlie!

Charlie   (*pretending to be surprised*) Oh, it's you, Vera.

Vera   Yes, it's me, Charlie. (*she holds up a chart and tries not to smile*) What is the meaning of this? (*the chart has a huge Smilie face drawn on it*) And this?

She holds up another which has very exaggerated peaks and troughs in the graph.

Charlie   Ah . . .

Vera   (*pretending to be cross*) Well, I'm waiting.

Louise enters.

Louise   Staff, there's a group of lads outside wanting to see Charlie.

Vera   Oh, yes, I know about them. They'd better come in then.

She shakes her head but can't help smiling.

Vera   Saved by the bell, young man, but don't think you've heard the last of this!

She throws the charts down on his bed, and she and Louise go out. He snatches up the charts and stuffs them in the waste-paper bin. Ben, Femi, Robert and Hugo enter.

Ben   Hey, Charlie, all right?

Robert   It's like Fort Knox trying to get into here.

Charlie   I know, I couldn't have visitors for ages.

Hugo   They said you were really ill and we thought you were going to –

Ben   Shut it, Hugo.

Hugo   Yeah, sorry. Anyway, it's great to see you're better. You glad to see us?

Charlie   You bet, even you, de la Haye. It's been dead boring.

Femi   When are you coming out?

Charlie   Soon, I hope. Otherwise, I'll just walk out.

Ben   You can't do that.

Charlie   Watch me. Hey look at this!

He puts on a wig and a hat, then some more and throws them at the boys who try them on too and throw them around the room shouting and laughing. There is mayhem as Louise enters. Hugo collides with her knocking a surgical tray out of her hands. The clatter makes everybody freeze.

Louise   What on earth's going on in here? If you boys can't behave you'll have to leave.

Charlie   Don't be a spoilsport, Louise, we were only having a laugh.

Charlie starts them off again. Louise shouts at them to stop but they ignore her. Hugo tries to get her attention by helping her to pick up the things.

She thanks him and the others jeer at him. Louise goes out and returns with Vera who comes into the room with such presence that they all stop misbehaving immediately.

Vera Charlie, I've a good mind to send your friends home and confiscate your television!

Charlie Oh, don't do that, Vera. We'll behave, I promise.

Femi Sorry, Nurse, it was our fault.

Vera Charlie has been very ill. He needs rest, not a riot.

Hugo Sorry.

Charlie Aw, Vera, they didn't mean anything. We just got carried away.

Vera You have been warned – and next time don't ignore Louise.

Robert Hugo wasn't ignoring her!

They laugh at this and then look suitably sorry. The nurses go out and they burst out laughing again. Frances enters in her wheelchair. The boys stare.

Frances What's going on? Staff's really angry.

Charlie Nothing much. They never let you have any fun in this place. Everybody, this is Frances. (*he introduces his friends*) Ben, Femi, Robert, Hugo.

They all say hello to one another.

Frances So, what were you doing?

Ben Sort of American football with wigs.

Frances Typical boys.

Robert You been in here long?

Frances Years, on and off.

Robert That must be really boring.

Frances You get used to it.

Hugo How long have you got to be in that thing for?

Charlie Watch it, Hugo.

Hugo   Sorry, didn't mean to be rude.

Frances For ever.

Femi   (*shocked*) Oh. Have you always been like that?

Ben   Femi, shut up, will you?

Frances No, it's all right, honestly. It's nice to have someone talking about it for a change. Most people just ignore you. For the record, boys, I was born like this. OK?

Robert   Yeah, right.

Charlie Frances plays the violin really well.

Femi   Straight up? I wouldn't have thought . . . (*he stops in embarrassment*) . . . I mean . . .

Frances You mean, you wouldn't have thought 'cripples' like me could play a musical instrument?

Femi   No . . . I . . .

Frances It's all right. People do this to me all the time. They even turn to my mother, or a nurse and say, 'Does she do this or does she do that?' As though there's something wrong with my brain as well. Why don't they ask me? It's my legs that don't work, not my brain.

Femi   Yeah, right.

Charlie Hey, let's have a rave!

Ben   What, now?

Charlie Yeah, why not?

Frances Staff'll go mad, that's why.

Ben   Who cares? She'll only tell us to turn the music down. Right?

Robert   Or chuck us out!

Charlie No, Vera's all right really.

Charlie goes to his stereo unit and puts on some fast noisy music. The boys shout and dance.

Charlie I've got an idea. Hold on.

He goes out. Hugo whirls Frances round in her wheelchair.

Frances (*laughing*) Stop it, you'll make me sick.

Hugo Doesn't matter. The nurses'll come in and clear it up.

Frances You're the limit.

Hugo And you're all right, got that?

Frances (*meaning it*) Thanks, Hugo.

Charlie comes back with a skeleton.

Ben Where did you get that thing?

Charlie Treatment room. Here you are, Hugo. Pretend it's Catherine.

They look at each other for a moment then Charlie smiles and Hugo relaxes and dances with the skeleton, and they shout and cheer and fall about laughing. Vera enters and they are suddenly silent. Charlie turns the music down.

Vera Well, it hasn't taken you boys long to create absolute mayhem, has it? I've a good mind not to tell you the good news, Charlie.

Charlie Oh, Vera.

Vera But as it means getting rid of you I'll tell you now. You'll be going home in a few days.

The boys, especially Charlie, cheer. Frances turns her wheelchair round and steers away from them.

Vera Now, might I suggest for the peace and quiet of this ward, and before Sister comes on duty, that you all go off to the cafeteria and calm down.

Charlie Great!

Vera goes.

Ben That means you'll be back at school next week.

Charlie (*being sarcastic*) Oh, fantastic.

Robert We've got a new French assistant, Juliette. *Ooh la la.*

Femi   And old Llewellyn-Smith is retiring at the end of this year.

Charlie   About time too.

Femi   And –

Ben   Oh, come off it. Who cares? Let's go.

Charlie   You joining us, Frances?

Frances   (*with her back to them*) Yes, in a minute. I want to go to my locker first.

Charlie   OK, we'll get you something. What would you like?

Frances   Anything, I don't mind.

Charlie   OK, see you there in a minute. Hey, last one there buys!

              They all rush out. Frances stays, looking very down. She goes to Charlie's stereo, takes a CD from her pocket and puts on the second movement of Schubert's Piano Trio in B flat, *the Andante where the violin is heard. She listens to it and the tears come. After a while Charlie rushes in.*

Charlie   Frances, I thought you were coming to the –

              He stops as he sees what's happening. He goes to Frances and kneels down by her wheelchair so that he's at her height. He holds her hand.

Charlie   It's all right, you'll be going home soon.

Frances   I'm not better though, am I? Not like you. I'll always be like this.

Charlie   It doesn't matter. Not to me anyway. It's you that matters. I like you as you are. You're really nice, Frances, and you're ever so clever.

Frances   So what? I'd rather be stupid and be able to walk.

Charlie   I know, but sometimes we can't have what we want.

Frances   It's not fair.

Charlie   Nothing's fair. I've learned that. But you're still here and I'm still here and I'll keep in touch, I promise.

Frances   That's what everybody says and they never do.

Charlie   No, I mean it. (*quietly, intently*) I really like you, Frances. Honest. And I want to see you again if . . . if you want to see me.

Frances   (*looking at him in disbelief*) Really?

Charlie   Yes. Honest.

Frances   OK, then.

Charlie   (*relieved*) Great. I'll visit you here and bring the others.

Frances   (*pretending*) Oh, please, no!

Charlie   And you can come and visit me, at home or school. They'll let you. It's going to be all right, I promise.

Frances   Yes.

Charlie   Come on, smile, the others are waiting. (*he wipes her tears away*) I don't want them to see you like this.

Frances   (*brightening up*) OK.

Charlie   Come on then, I'll push you.

Frances   No thanks, I want to get there in one piece.

Charlie   I'll be careful.

Frances   Oh, all right.

He turns her wheelchair round and launches it off. As he is leaving Louise enters and they collide. She drops the clean laundry she's carrying.

Louise   Not again! And where are you two going?

Charlie   Sorry, can't stop. Urgent business.

Louise   Wait! Who's going to help me clear this up?

Charlie looks around then grabs hold of the skeleton and gives it to her.

Charlie Ask him. Though I shouldn't bank on it. He's
bone idle!

*Frances bursts out laughing. Charlie runs out
pushing the wheelchair and shouting with joy, 'Dem
bones, dem bones, dem dry bones!' Louise is left
standing alone holding the skeleton.*

The End

The Russian Bracelet

List of Characters

Girls
Julia
Sam
Donna
Jenny
Kerry
Leila
Yasmin

Adults
Mrs Altman, An Old Lady
Miss Barnes, Manager of Nursing Home
Mrs Simons, Julia's mother
Mr Simons, Julia's father
Mr Keane, Old Man
Mrs Fraser, Teacher
Mr Wynne-Jones, Old Man (Mr W-J)
Sgt Hawker
WPC Ndogala (WPC N)
Youth Leader
Narrator

THE RUSSIAN BRACELET

Scene One

Characters: Julia, Miss Barnes (Manager of Nursing Home), Mr Keane, Mrs Altman.

It is Sunday afternoon at a nursing home for the elderly and Julia is visiting Mrs Altman, one of its residents, as part of her community work for her Youth Group. Miss Barnes sees her come in.

Miss Barnes   Ah, hello, Julia. Nice to see you again. Mrs Altman is in the lounge waiting for you.

Julia   Thanks. I've got some of my artwork to show her. She's very interested in art. She told me that her uncle was an artist.

Miss Barnes   Yes, he was quite famous. Had a summer exhibition at the Royal Academy in London.

An old man shuffles up to them and talks to Julia.

Mr Keane   Where's me porridge?

Julia   What?

Mr Keane   Where's me porridge? What have you done with it?

Julia   Uh . . . nothing. I've come to visit Mrs Altman.

Miss Barnes   Now, Mr Keane, don't go bothering young Julia here. She's not one of the staff.

Mr Keane   (*to Miss Barnes*) Are you staff?

Miss Barnes   Yes, you know who I am. I'm Miss Barnes, the manager of this nursing home.

Mr Keane   I haven't had me porridge.

Miss Barnes   Yes, you have. You had porridge this morning for breakfast.

Mr Keane	I've had no lunch.
Miss Barnes	Yes, you did. You had your lunch only an hour ago.
Mr Keane	I missed that. I didn't get anything to eat.
Miss Barnes	No, you were at the table with all the others and had lovely roast beef.
Mr Keane	I don't like roast beef. I only like porridge. (*to Julia*) Where's me porridge?
Miss Barnes	(*steering him away*) Now come along, Mr Keane. Julia doesn't want to hear all this. I'll get Nurse McAteer to take you back to your room so you can have a nice rest. (*to Julia*) Sorry about this. He gets very confused sometimes. You go and see Mrs Altman.

Julia goes into the lounge where Mrs Altman is sitting by the window. When she sees Julia she smiles.

Mrs Altman	Hello, dear. You made it then?
Julia	Yes, Mum didn't need me to help after all.
Mrs Altman	That's good. I really look forward to your visits, you know. It's so dull otherwise.
Julia	Don't you like it in here?
Mrs Altman	Oh, it's fine but I get a bit fed up with the same people all the time. It's nice to see a different face, especially a young one like yours. And some of them are . . . well . . . I don't mean to be rude, but a bit past it.
Julia	Yes, I know what you mean. Mr Keane kept asking me where I'd put his porridge.
Mrs Altman	Don't you take any notice of him. Yesterday it was his toast and he pestered us about it all day but he's harmless really, poor man. He's got worse lately. He doesn't remember anything from one minute to the next. He keeps looking for his wife but she died years ago.
Julia	That's horrible.

Mrs Altman   Not really, dear. He's quite happy in his own little world. It's just irritating for the rest of us sometimes. Now, did you get those sweets I asked for?

Julia   Yes, I've got them in my bag. (*she takes out the sweets and hands them to Mrs Altman*) Mint humbugs, just what you asked for, though it took me ages to find a shop that sells them.

Mrs Altman   They don't make decent sweets any more, not the old-fashioned ones like they used to. It's all crisps and McDonald's nowadays. When I was a child we used to have gobstoppers, and bullseyes, and twirly sticks, and sherbet lemons. Oh, they were lovely and you could get ever so many with a few coppers.

Julia   Mum says they're bad for your teeth.

Mrs Altman   Oh, go on! They never did me any harm.

Julia   Haven't you got false teeth then?

Mrs Altman   (*pretending to be shocked*) Here, do you mind! As a matter of fact, I have but that's nothing to do with the sweeties we had in the old days.

Miss Barnes passes by as Mrs Altman pops a mint humbug into her mouth and offers one to Julia. She tuts in disapproval.

Miss Barnes   Mrs Altman, I hope you're not leading Julia into bad ways – and you're not getting one of those stuck in your false teeth again. We had a terrible time getting it unstuck last time. It nearly broke them.

Mrs Altman   Don't remind me. I wouldn't have been able to eat my lamb chop if that'd happened.

Miss Barnes   (*laughing*) Nothing would keep you from your lamb chops, Mrs Altman!

Miss Barnes goes.

Mrs Altman   Now, Julia, tell me all about this music concert you're doing at school and then we'll look at your artwork.

Scene Two

Characters: Sam, Julia.

Julia has left the nursing home and is walking home when Sam, a girl who goes to the same school as Julia, comes alongside her. Julia is obviously frightened. Sam walks beside her for a bit, making faces and imitating the way she walks, then steps in front of Julia forcing her to stop.

Sam Been somewhere, have we, Jules?

Julia Yes, I've been visiting Mrs Altman – and my name's Julia, not Jules.

Sam (*giving her a push*) It's whatever I want to call you, OK? Anyway, what you hanging about for?

Julia I'm not. I was on my way home till . . . (*she stops*)

Sam Yeah, go on. Till?

Julia Till you got in my way.

Sam I'm not in your way. You can go any time. Go on, go.

Julia (*tries to move but Sam blocks her way each time*) I can't, you're in the way.

Sam No, I'm not. Go on.

Julia I can't.

Sam You calling me a liar?

Julia No.

Sam Yes, you are. I don't like people calling me a liar, OK? (*Julia doesn't answer*) So what you visiting this old lady for then?

Julia She doesn't have any family so I go and see her and keep her company.

Sam You after her money?

Julia (*indignant*) No!

Sam Oh, come off it. No one visits old wrinklies 'cos they like it.

Julia Well, we do. Everyone at our Youth Group does community work.

Sam *Youth Group?* Stupid! You only do it to try and pretend you're better than anyone else.

Julia No we don't.

Sam You arguing with me? (*Julia doesn't answer*) Stuck-up toffee-nosed git. Think you're so great, doing community work.

Julia Leave me alone.

Sam Don't tell me you're not after something from that old lady.

Julia I'm not.

Sam Liar.

Julia Just leave me alone, will you?

Sam I might, if you make it worth my while. Know what I mean?

Julia I haven't got any more money, if that's what you're talking about.

Sam Why not? I told you you hadn't given me enough.

Julia That's all I get.

Sam Well, you'd better get some more.

Julia Where am I supposed to get it from? I only get the pocket money my mum gives me and you had that on Friday.

Sam (*threatening her*) Listen, Jules, I don't care where you get it from. That's your problem, right? Get it from that old lady. She must have stacks if she's living at that posh home. So just get it, OK?

Julia (*nearly in tears*) Yes, yes all right.

Sam Good, 'cos if you don't, you know what's going to happen, don't you?

Sam walks off laughing. Julia is shaking and waits until Sam is out of sight before hurrying off home.

Scene Three

Characters: Mr Simons, Mrs Simons.
At the Simons' home later that evening. Julia's
parents are drinking coffee in their lounge.

Mr Simons	So what did you want to speak to me about, Ruth? Are you still worried about Julia?
Mrs Simons	Yes, she's really getting on my nerves.
Mr Simons	How do you mean?
Mrs Simons	Well, she's been very secretive lately and gets all moody when I want to talk to her.
Mr Simons	Now, you're not trying to tell me that a teenager is being moody, are you?
Mrs Simons	No, listen, I think she's been taking money out of my purse.
Mr Simons	This sounds serious. What's been happening?
Mrs Simons	Well, she's been asking for extra pocket money recently and when I try to question her about what she wants it for, she's very cagey.
Mr Simons	You mean, you think she's up to something?
Mrs Simons	I don't know for sure. It's just a feeling I've got.
Mr Simons	Maybe it's not as bad as you think, Ruth. You know what they're like at her age. We went through it all with Rebecca. Make-up, and clothes, and CDs – not to mention boyfriends.
Mrs Simons	I don't think it's that. You see, she came home from her visit to Mrs Altman this afternoon looking very upset. Wouldn't have any tea, wouldn't speak except to say that it was nothing to do with Mrs Altman. Then she asked me for extra pocket money.
Mr Simons	How much?

Mrs Simons	Five pounds. When I said 'no' she threw a tantrum. I'm the worst mother in the world. Why can't she be treated like everyone else in the family. All her friends have loads more pocket money than she does. Then she stormed off upstairs, went straight to her room and stayed there. The door's locked and she won't let me in.
Mr Simons	So you think she's in some sort of trouble?
Mrs Simons	It looks like it. Yes.
Mr Simons	Maybe she's fallen out with someone at school. You know what it's like. One of her friends is probably friends with somebody else and she's jealous.
Mrs Simons	No, it's definitely something to do with money, Howard. Just before you came in I went to look for my diary in my handbag. I'd left the bag in the bedroom but when I opened it I noticed that my purse was open and five pounds was missing.
Mr Simons	Are you sure?
Mrs Simons	Yes, and it's not the first time that money's gone missing – and she did ask me for an extra five pounds.
Mr Simons	Have you spoken to her about it?
Mrs Simons	No, I told you. She's locked herself in her bedroom and won't let me in. I think you should try to speak to her. You know how she is with me at the moment. I can't say a word without her flying off the handle and telling me I'm on her back all the time. Honestly, Howard, it's all getting too much. I am really worried about her.
Mr Simons	Right, I'll have a word. But listen, Ruth, if there's one thing we can say about Julia, she's totally honest. She'd never take anything – not from you, not from anybody. You know that.
Mrs Simons	Oh, I suppose so but I'd still like you to find out what's going on. She's better with you. I just seem to wind her up all the time.
Mr Simons	OK, I'll go up and speak to her now.

Scene Four

Characters: Mr Simons, Julia.

Julia is in her bedroom lying on the bed listening to a CD. Her dad knocks on the door.

Mr Simons Hi, can I have a word? (*Julia doesn't answer*) Please, darling, it's really important. (*joking*) I won't let Mum in!

Julia Oh, all right.

Julia reluctantly unlocks the door and then flops down on the bed.

Mr Simons Um . . . can we have that music off? I can hardly hear myself think.

Julia sulkily snaps a button on her remote control.

Mr Simons Hey, I only asked! Come on, what's up?

Julia Nothing.

Mr Simons Not according to your mother.

Julia Oh, yeah, what have I done now?

Mr Simons I think you were a bit short with her when you came home from Mrs Altman's.

Julia Nothing I ever do is right for her!

Mr Simons Now you know that's not true. She's very concerned about you.

Julia So?

Mr Simons You're not making this very easy for me, Henny.

Julia Don't call me that stupid name! I'm not a kid any more.

Mr Simons Sorry, I keep forgetting. I keep thinking you're still my little girl. I can't bear to think of you growing up so fast. (*pause*) Come on, what's all this about you and Mum?

Julia	Dad, she's always on at me, asking me what I'm doing, where I'm going, who I'm with. It's none of her business. Doesn't she trust me or something?
Mr Simons	Ah, well, I was coming to that. Apparently you've been asking for a lot of extra pocket money lately.
Julia	So?
Mr Simons	So, what's your reason?
	Julia says nothing; her dad gets more serious.
Mr Simons	I want an answer, Julia.
Julia	I've just had a lot of extra things to buy lately, that's all. All the other girls in my class get far more than I do. What's the big deal?
Mr Simons	Well, if you really need an increase in pocket money then we can discuss it. But that's not all, is it? Mum told me that you'd asked for extra this afternoon and now she's got five pounds missing from her purse.
Julia	(*getting up angrily*) Oh, yeah, it's got to be me, right? I always get the blame, don't I? What about Tim? He could have taken it.
Mr Simons	Tim's not back from rugby yet.
Julia	Well, Becky then.
Mr Simons	She's round at Caroline's.
Julia	That's it. Go on, blame me. I always get the blame for everything, don't I? Not Becky. She's too sensible. Not Tim. He's too goody-goody.
Mr Simons	Julia, nobody's blaming you. Nobody's accusing you. I merely said that money was missing.
Julia	Yeah, well, it wasn't me, right? It wasn't me!
	Julia runs out, slamming the door. Her father runs after her.
Mr Simons	Julia, come back!

Scene Five

Characters: Donna, Sam, Julia, Mrs Fraser.

At school the next day. It's break-time. Sam and her friend Donna have cornered Julia behind a stairwell, out of sight of anyone else.

Donna   Shall I keep a lookout, Sam?

Sam   Yeah, give us a shout if anyone's coming.

Donna   Right, and give us a shout too if there's any bother.

Sam   (*right in Julia's face*) Oh, there won't be. (*Donna moves away*) Right, Jules, you got that dosh?

Julia   Yes. (*she takes a five-pound note out of her pocket and gives it to Sam*) But I can't get any more.

Sam   (*snatching the money*) Listen, you, I'll decide what you can and can't get, dummy. Right?

She pushes Julia against the wall as Julia puts her arms up to defend herself.

Sam   Something wrong, Jules? Eh? Eh?

Julia   No.

Sam   Great. Just so you understand. And no grassing, you little snitch, 'cos I can get you any time. Isn't that right, Donna?

Donna   Yeah, she knows what she'll get if she grasses.

Julia   Look, it's no good asking me for any more money until my pocket money on Friday. I can't get any more. My mum and dad think I pinched that money from them and they're watching me.

Sam   That's your problem, stupid. We don't care where you get it from. Still, this should just about last us till Friday – but no messing me about after that. Got it?

Julia   Yes.

Donna   Ask your old lady for some more pocket money. She can afford it. Your parents are loaded.

Julia   No, they're not.

Sam   You arguing with us?

Julia   No.

Sam   Yes, you are. Don't get lippy with me.

Donna   Sam, Mrs Fraser's coming!

Sam   OK. (*to Julia menacingly as she takes some gum out of her mouth and sticks it on Julia's blazer lapel*) Remember what I said, right? Ugh, you stink! Come on, Donna, let's get out of here.

Sam and Donna disappear quickly. Julia is shaking and stays where she is trying not cry. She takes a tissue out her pocket and removes the gum.
Mrs Fraser appears.

Mrs Fraser   Who's hiding away around here? Oh, Julia it's you. What are you doing here?

Julia   Nothing, just going, Mrs Fraser.

Mrs Fraser   Everything all right? Only I thought I just saw Sam and her crony, Donna, beetling off down the corridor.

Julia   No, Mrs Fraser, I'm fine.

Mrs Fraser   You don't have to put up with any unpleasantness, you know. This school has a clear policy on bullying.

Julia   I'm all right.

Mrs Fraser   (*doubtful*) Hmm, well you can always come and tell me if anything's wrong. Or any of the other teachers.

Julia   Yes, Mrs Fraser.

Julia stands awkwardly. The bell goes.

Mrs Fraser   There, saved by the bell. Off you go.

Julia gratefully slips away. Mrs Fraser watches her and frowns.

Mrs Fraser   (*to herself*) Hmm, I think this one needs watching. Sam Clark isn't the type who Julia Simons normally hangs around with.

Scene Six

Characters: Miss Barnes, Julia.

The nursing home after school a week later. Miss Barnes has asked to see Julia in her office. Julia enters after knocking on the door.

Miss Barnes   Ah, there you are, Julia. Come in, dear, and sit down. Now, you visited Mrs Altman yesterday.

Julia   Yes.

Miss Barnes   How are you getting on with her?

Julia   Really well. She's very interesting to talk to.

Miss Barnes   Yes, she's a very intelligent old lady. That's why she needs someone like you who's bright and can talk about the things she likes. Most of the residents here she finds rather boring. She's got a great sense of humour. I think she might have been a bit wild in her younger days.

Julia   I know. She can be quite a laugh sometimes.

Miss Barnes   (*getting more serious*) Julia, did Mrs Altman ask you to go to her room for anything yesterday?

Julia   Yes, she asked me to fetch her cardigan. She was feeling a bit cold.

Miss Barnes   And . . . ah . . . while you were there you didn't touch anything or look around?

Julia   No, why should I?

Miss Barnes   Do you know that Mrs Altman has a lot of jewellery?

Julia   Well, I know she's quite rich. The watch and brooches and stuff she wears are all really expensive.

Miss Barnes   Yes, but do you know that there are other items in her room?

Julia   No, I mean she's never told me.

Miss Barnes   And you've never been tempted to look and see?

Julia   No, I wouldn't dream of looking round. Her things are private. What's this all about? Am I supposed to have taken something?

Miss Barnes   Let me get this straight. Nobody's accusing you of anything yet but yesterday afternoon, after you'd gone, Mrs Altman went back to her room and found that her things had been disturbed.

Julia   What things?

Miss Barnes   Well, her jewellery actually.

Julia   I didn't touch anything, I swear. I mean, I was only in there for a few seconds. I got her cardi on the bed and came straight out of her room.

Miss Barnes   Yes, I'm sure that you did but, you see, something very, very valuable has gone missing from Mrs Altman's room. (*Julia looks very shocked*) We're not panicking just yet. And don't think I'm accusing you. We all know you're very trustworthy here. Old people do forget where they've put things and it may come to light. But if it doesn't we shall have to call in the police. It's too valuable to go missing. For the time being I'm just trying to establish who had access to her room yesterday.

Julia   Well, I didn't take anything – I mean, only her cardigan.

Miss Barnes   Good. (*getting up*) Well, I'm sure there's some perfectly reasonable explanation and it'll be found in some unlikely place like the wardrobe or wherever. We're always having these kinds of panics with the residents. As I said, they're very elderly and they forget easily. Anyway, that's enough for the time being. You'd better run along and see Mrs Altman. She always looks forward to your visits.

Julia nods and goes.

Scene Seven

Characters: Mrs Altman, Julia, Mr Wynne-Jones.

Julia is feeling rather sick but she still decides to see Mrs Altman. She goes to the lounge where the old lady is standing by the bookcase.

Mrs Altman   Hello, Julia dear, it's so nice to see you again. I'm trying to find a decent book but they're all 'penny dreadfuls' here, as my mother would say. No Tolstoy or Chekov. Anyway, come and sit down, dear, you look awfully pale. Is there anything the matter?

Julia   I've just seen Miss Barnes. She said that something very valuable had gone missing from your room.

Mrs Altman   Oh, that! Don't you worry yourself, my dear. I told them it couldn't possibly be you. You're far too well bred for that. 'Not Julia, she's too honest,' I told them. Besides, it'll probably be found tomorrow in some unlikely place such as the laundry basket.

Julia   That's what Miss Barnes said.

Mrs Altman   And she's quite right, so don't you go getting upset, my dear.

They go and sit down.

Julia   What went missing?

Mrs Altman   Well, it was a bracelet given to my mother by Czarina Alexandra – you know the Russian royal family were called the Romanovs and she was the wife of Czar Nicholas who ruled Russia just before the Revolution in 1917. My parents managed to escape with me – I was a baby then – and came to England. My father was a Count, you see, and would have been killed by the Bolsheviks. Anyway, my mother was one of the Czarina's

maids-in-waiting. Alexandra was very fond of my
mother and gave her the bracelet as a wedding gift.
It's got diamonds and things all over it. I wouldn't be
that fussed really only it belonged to my darling
mother whom I adored and it's of great sentimental
value to me. I'm not interested in its money value.
And it's my own fault. I should have asked Miss
Barnes to put it back in the safe.

Julia Is that where it's always kept?

Mrs Altman Yes, it is rather silly to have such valuable items in
one's room.

Julia Why did you have it?

Mrs Altman Well, the day before was my mother's birthday and
I simply wanted to be near it. You know, it seems to
bring her closer to me. She's been dead since I was
45 but I still think of her every day. I adored her so
much, you see.

Julia Didn't you put it back after?

Mrs Altman No, I meant to but I put it in my top drawer for
safety until I could find Miss Barnes and then I
promptly forgot. Oh well, that's enough of my
troubles, dear. Tell me what's happening at school.

*Mr Wynne-Jones has entered the room and goes
over to them. He points to Julia's chair with his
walking stick.*

Mr W-J That's Mr Regan's chair.

Mrs Altman (*irritably*) It's not anyone's chair, Mr Wynne-Jones.
Miss Barnes says we can sit anywhere we like in
this room.

Mr W-J He won't like it.

Mrs Altman Well, he'll have to lump it.

Julia It's all right, I'll move.

Mrs Altman (*holding out her hand*) You'll do nothing of the sort!
Mr Wynne-Jones, I am having a private conversation
with my little friend here. Do you mind?

Mr W-J   (*going away grumbling*) Well, he won't like it.
                Whatever next? Visitors taking residents' chairs. I
                don't know.

Mrs Altman (*indignant*) Oh, he's such a rude man. And his table
                manners are revolting! Bit like him really.

                Mrs Altman laughs wickedly and Julia smiles.

Scene Eight

*Characters: Mrs Simons, Julia, WPC Ndogala,
Sgt Hawker, Mr Simons.*

*It is several days later. Julia arrives home from
school to find a police car parked outside her house
and her mother anxiously waiting on the doorstep.*

Julia   (*worried*) What's up?

Mrs Simons The police are here. They want to talk to you.

Julia   Me? Why?

Mrs Simons I think you know why.

Julia   What? Just because you think I took five pounds
                from your purse?

Mrs Simons Of course not. What do you take me for? It's much
                more serious than that. (*whispering*) Tell me now,
                Julia, if you've done anything wrong.

Julia   Oh, yeah, you really do trust me, don't you, Mum?

Mrs Simons Julia!

                *Julia glares at her mother, then marches into the
                lounge, followed closely by her mother. The two
                police officers stand up and introduce themselves.*

Sgt Hawker I'm Sergeant Hawker.

WPC N   WPC Ndogala.

Sgt Hawker   Sit down, please, Julia. We've got one or two questions to ask you. We'd like your mum to stay while we do so, please.

Mrs Simons   I've no intentions of going. I'd like to know what all this is about, Sergeant.

Sgt Hawker   All in good time, Mrs Simons.

WPC N   Can you first confirm that you are Julia Simons?

Julia   Yes.

WPC N   (*writing in her notebook*) And you do normally live at this address?

Julia   Yes.

Sgt Hawker   Julia, do you know why we're here? (*Julia shakes her head*) Do you know a Mrs Altman?

Julia   Yes, I visit her at the nursing home. Is this about her missing bracelet?

Mrs Simons   What?

WPC N   Yes, it is, I'm afraid.

Julia   (*getting upset*) I didn't touch it. I didn't take it. I've never even seen it! Mum!

Mrs Simons   It's all right, darling, just calm down.

Sgt Hawker   If you haven't taken it, Julia, then there's nothing to worry about.

Julia   Oh, no? Bet everybody thinks I did by now. Even Mrs Altman.

WPC N   If it's any consolation to you, she did tell us that she didn't think you would ever do such a thing.

Sgt Hawker   But we do have routine enquiries to make and we need to make sure that you weren't involved.

Julia   (*shouting*) I wasn't! Why doesn't anyone believe me?

Mrs Simons   Keep calm, darling. If you've done nothing wrong there's nothing to worry about.

Sgt Hawker	We'd like to take a look at your room if we may?
Julia	No!
Mrs Simons	(*warning her*) Julia.
Sgt Hawker	We do have a search warrant. Show Mrs Simons, Jean. (*the WPC shows the warrant*) Knowing your husband is a solicitor we've made sure everything is above board.
Mrs Simons	I bet you have.
WPC N	We won't take long and we'll be as careful as we can not to disturb anything.
Mrs Simons	It's upstairs, turn left on the landing and it's the door right at the end.
WPC N	Thank you.
	They go out. Julia is very agitated and tries to go after them but her mother holds her back.
Mrs Simons	No, they'll call you up if they want you.
Julia	But, Mum, they'll see all my private things. I've got my diary and everything up there.
Mrs Simons	There's nothing we can do about it.
	Julia looks very depressed. Mrs Simons gives her a hug.
Mrs Simons	Don't worry. Dad will sort this out. I'm sure it's all been a dreadful mistake. (*unsure*) It is, isn't it, Julia?
	Julia looks at her mother in disbelief. They hear the front door opening and Mr Simons comes hurrying in. Julia runs up to him.
Julia	Dad!
Mr Simons	(*giving her a hug*) Steady on. (*to Mrs Simons*) What's going on?
Mrs Simons	Howard, thank goodness you're home. This is a nightmare. The police are searching Julia's room.
Mr Simons	Whatever for?
Julia	They think I've stolen Mrs Altman's bracelet.

Mr Simons	(*to Mrs Simons*) Who's here?
Mrs Simons	A Sergeant Hawker –
Mr Simons	Ah, Liz Hawker. I know her very well. She's good. She'll go by the book. Anyway, they know me so they wouldn't try it on. Who's she with?
Mrs Simons	WPC Ndogala.
Julia	Dad, what are they going to do?
Mr Simons	It depends. Just tell me one thing, Julia, and don't take it the wrong way, but the police aren't going to find anything in your room that they shouldn't, are they?
Julia	No, of course not!
Mr Simons	Good, then you've got nothing to worry about. They may think you've done it but if they can't prove it – if there's no material evidence as it's called, which means if they can't find the stolen goods – then it's all circumstantial and you have no case to answer.
Mrs Simons	This is ridiculous. Whatever will the neighbours think?
Mr Simons	Who cares what they think? They're the least of our worries at the moment.
Mrs Simons	And there's your position to think of, Howard. You're a solicitor for heaven's sake! You can't afford a scandal. Your own child being accused of theft! Oh, I can't stand this waiting. I'm going to get a cup of tea.
	She goes to the kitchen.
Julia	(*tearful*) Dad, what's going to happen now?
Mr Simons	Well, if they don't find anything in your room they may leave it at that but I suspect that because it's such a serious matter they may want to ask you some questions at the station.
Julia	No!
Mr Simons	It's all right. I'll be there.
Julia	Mum doesn't believe me, does she?
	Mr Simons doesn't answer.

Scene Nine

*Characters: Sgt Hawker, WPC Ndogala, Julia,
Mr Simons.*

*At the police station later. Julia is in the Interview
Room with her father.*

Sgt Hawker Right, Julia, we are recording this interview with
you. Do you understand what that means?

WPC N It means that we can't say you said anything you
didn't, if it's all down on tape.

Julia Yes, I know.

Sgt Hawker OK, let's begin. How long have you been visiting
Mrs Altman?

Julia About six months.

Sgt Hawker Did you know her before?

Julia No.

Sgt Hawker So she isn't a relative? A friend of the family?

Julia No.

WPC N So how come you started visiting her?

Julia Well, I belong to a Youth Group –

Sgt Hawker Which one?

Julia Mount Pleasant.

Sgt Hawker Go on.

Julia Well, we have projects there like it's for sport, or
drama, and stuff, and you can choose them but
everyone has to do a community project. It's
compulsory.

WPC N Does everybody do the same thing? Like old
people's homes, I mean?

Julia No, you can choose anything you want.

Sgt Hawker So why did you choose an old people's home?

Julia	I like old people. Both my grandmothers live a long way away and I really miss them so I thought it'd be great to visit someone old.
WPC N	But if you've got grannies of your own, Julia, why do want to see more old people?
Julia	I've told you. I like old people. I get on really well with them.
WPC N	Is it because they're an easy target?
Julia	What?
WPC N	For stealing, Julia.
Julia	No!
WPC N	All right, I'll put it another way. If you were intending to steal from somebody wouldn't you want to make it as easy as possible?
Mr Simons	That's a leading question, WPC Ndogala. You don't have to answer that, Julia.
Julia	I want to answer. I don't know about it being easy. I've never stolen anything.
WPC N	So you don't think that old people are forgetful and wouldn't notice anything missing?
	Julia starts to speak but her dad cuts in.
Mr Simons	She's already answered that question. She doesn't have to answer it again.
Sgt Hawker	OK, let's move on. Tell us what happened on the afternoon that Mrs Altman's bracelet went missing.
Julia	Well, I visited her as usual after Sunday lunch.
WPC N	What time was that?
Julia	About half-past two.
WPC N	Right.
Julia	And we went into the main lounge –
Sgt Hawker	Were there any other residents in there?
Julia	Yes, quite a few.
Sgt Hawker	Go on.

Julia	Then Mrs Altman asked me to fetch her cardigan from her room as she was cold.
Sgt Hawker	What time was this?
Julia	I don't know. About three, I think. So I went and got it.
WPC N	Did anyone see you go into the room?
Julia	I don't know.
WPC N	A member of staff, perhaps?
Mr Simons	My daughter has just told you she doesn't know.
WPC N	But she might remember, Mr Simons.
Mr Simons	She's answered your question once. She does not have to answer it again.
Sgt Hawker	OK. Julia, did you know that Mrs Altman had a lot of jewellery?
Julia	Yes.
Sgt Hawker	And did you know it was very valuable?
Julia	Yes. No. Well, I mean I didn't know. I just thought it looked expensive.
Sgt Hawker	And did you know about the bracelet?
Julia	Yes.
Sgt Hawker	So you knew what it looked like and –
Julia	No, no, I'd never seen it before.
Sgt Hawker	But you've just said you had.
Julia	No, I didn't mean that. I meant not before it was stolen.
WPC N	Does that mean that you saw it after it was stolen?
Julia	No, no, I've never seen it. I didn't know anything about it until after.
Sgt Hawker	But you just said you knew all about it, Julia.
Julia	I got confused. Mrs Altman told me about the bracelet afterwards.
WPC N	Are you sure it was afterwards and not before?

Julia	Yes.
WPC N	Which, Julia?
Julia	I mean it was before – no, I mean after. Look, you're confusing me.
Sgt Hawker	Is that because you're getting flustered, Julia? Changing your story to make it look better?
Julia	No, no, I've told you!
Sgt Hawker	Did you plan this, or was it on the spur of the moment?
Julia	I didn't plan anything!
WPC N	We quite understand, Julia, if temptation came your way.
Julia	I wasn't tempted.
WPC N	You might have snatched it up and then realised what you had done later and tried to hide it, pretend you knew nothing about it.
Julia	No, no, it wasn't like that!
Sgt Hawker	What was it like then?
Julia	Nothing, I didn't do anything.
WPC N	Come on, Julia, if it was just on the spur of the moment, we understand. It could happen to anybody.
Julia	I've said it wasn't. Why do you keep asking me?
Mr Simons	Sergeant Hawker, I would like to remind you about harassing my daughter.
Sgt Hawker	We're just trying to establish the facts, Mr Simons. Julia doesn't seem to be too sure of them herself.
Julia	(*jumping up and shouting*) Look, I didn't do it! OK? I wouldn't steal from Mrs Altman. I would never do that! Why won't anybody believe me!
	Julia is in tears. She tries to run out of the room. WPC Ndogala intercepts her.
WPC N	OK, OK, Julia. Calm down. You can't leave yet.

| Mr Simons | I think we should take a break, Sergeant, in view of my daughter's distress. |
| Sgt Hawker | OK, we'll stop for fifteen minutes. |

Scene Ten

Characters: Mrs Simons, Mr Simons.
Later that evening. Julia's parents are discussing the day's events.

Mrs Simons	So she didn't actually admit anything?
Mr Simons	No, but it did look at one stage as though she was lying, or trying to cover up.
Mrs Simons	Oh, Howard.
Mr Simons	But that was because she got very flustered and confused, Ruth. It can be really frightening being questioned by the police, especially if it's never happened before. You say things you don't mean.
Mrs Simons	I thought that was why you were supposed to be there.
Mr Simons	I was there as her father and her solicitor, Ruth. I couldn't answer for her. I could only see that the police were being fair and acting by the book.
Mrs Simons	Sounds to me as though they weren't.
Mr Simons	No, I think they had to assume that Julia was guilty and they questioned her accordingly.
Mrs Simons	I thought we'd brought our children up to be decent and honest and now look what's happened.
Mr Simons	Listen, Ruth, Julia has got enough people assuming she's done this without us thinking it too. (*he pauses*) Oh, no, you don't really think she did it, do you?

Mrs Simons   I'm sorry but that's the way it looks to me. You know she was stealing money out of my purse and yet she flatly denied it. How am I suposed to believe her over this? She obviously needed money for something. Goodness knows what. We provide her with everything she needs and how does she repay us – by bringing shame and disgrace on this family.

Mr Simons   That's a bit hard, isn't it?

Mrs Simons   Maybe but I've had enough! It's the lies I can't stand. We've always told the children that no matter what they've done if they tell the truth the consequences will not be as bad as if they told lies. Fat lot of good that did.

Mr Simons   We're still her parents. We have to stand by her.

Mrs Simons   Well, you can stand by her if you like. I'm not doing another thing for her until she starts telling the truth.

Julia has been listening to this outside the door and when she hears her mother's last comment she opens the front door and runs off.

Scene Eleven

Characters: Julia, Youth Leader, Jenny, Kerry, Leila, Yasmin.

Julia arrives at the Youth Group's weekly meeting. As she enters the other girls, who are already there, whisper.

Leila   Look who's just walked in.

Kerry   What's she doing here?

Yasmin   She's got as much right to be here as you have.

Kerry	Well, I'm watching my purse while she's around.
Jenny	Don't be so horrible.
Leila	You can't tell me she didn't do it. My mum's a cook at that old lady's home and they all know she took that bracelet.
Yasmin	Saw her do it, did they?
Kerry	Oh, come off it, Yas, who else did it?
Jenny	There's people working there, aren't there?
Leila	My mum said it's more than their job's worth for the staff to take even a piece of fruit at the home, and they certainly wouldn't be stupid enough to nick the old people's stuff.
Youth Leader	(*shouting*) OK, everybody, two minutes and we'll get started. Report first, so be ready.
Jenny	Careful, she's coming over.
Yasmin	Oh hi, Julia. All right?
Julia	Yes, why shouldn't I be?
Kerry	Sorry, but we've got everybody we need in this group at the moment. Why don't you try Webster's?
Yasmin	Kerry!
Julia	No, it's all right. I'll see if Webster needs anyone.
	She goes.
Jenny	You didn't have to be so obvious, did you?
Kerry	We don't need her sort hanging around.
Leila	We've got ourselves to think of, Jenny. She could be nicking our stuff next.

Scene Twelve

Characters: Julia, Sam.

It is dark. Julia is on her way home on her own. Sam steps out of the shadows.

Sam   Evening, Jules. Where you off to then?

Julia   Home.

Sam   I hear you've been having a spot of bother. Oh dear, little Miss Perfect been up to naughty things, eh? Thieving. Told you, didn't I, that you were after that old wrinkly's money. And you're always pretending you're so great.

Julia   I didn't steal anything from her.

Sam   No, 'course not. Honest as the day's long, aren't you? But that's not what the police think. Yeah, and you only got off because your old man's a solicitor. People like you are all the same. Makes my guts ache. If it'd been me they wouldn't have let me off. But then, I'm from Ashley flats, aren't I?

Julia   That's because you would have done it.

Sam   (*getting aggressive*) What? What did you say? (*she starts to push Julia around*) Just watch it, all right, or you won't be walking home.

Julia   Why don't you leave me alone?

Sam   Because you're pathetic, and a stinking little swot, and all stuck-up and I hate you. That enough for you? Anyway, I'll let you go in a minute but there's something I want you to do first.

Julia   I'm not doing anything more for you. You can do it yourself!

Sam   Oh, yeah? We'll see about that.

Julia   I mean it.

Sam laughs at her.

Scene Thirteen

Characters: Miss Barnes, Julia, Mrs Altman.

The nursing home some days later. Julia enters and is seen by Miss Barnes who comes rushing over.

Miss Barnes Julia Simons! You've got a nerve. What do you think you're doing here? Don't think you're going to skip off with any more of the residents' possessions.

Mrs Altman (*moving to them as fast as she can*) She's here because I asked her to come, that's why. And don't you dare speak to a visitor of mine like that! Whatever next!

Julia I'd better go, Mrs Altman.

Mrs Altman Certainly not! You've done nothing wrong, dear – (*she glares at Miss Barnes*) – despite the efforts of some to prove otherwise.

Miss Barnes Really, Mrs Altman, you go too far sometimes. All right, she may stay for half an hour but she must remain in the lounge at all times with you and be escorted off the premises by myself or a member of my staff. Is that clear?

Mrs Altman Absurd! Come along, my dear, we'll go and take tea in the lounge and I shall chain you to the floor. (*she laughs and indicates Miss Barnes' retreating figure*) Silly old bat!

Scene Fourteen

Character: a Narrator for the stage directions.

Narrator It's the following evening. Julia arrives home and sneaks up to her room. She carefully locks the door and waits, listening. When she's satisfied she's safe she takes a chair and puts it by the wardrobe and stands on it, reaches up to the top of the wardrobe and pulls out something behind it wrapped in a cloth. She puts the chair back and sits on the bed. She opens out the cloth to reveal Mrs Altman's bracelet. The diamonds glitter in the lamplight. She picks it up and stares at it, tears in her eyes. Then she wraps it up and puts it in the top pocket of her denim jacket and buttons it up. She goes to her door and unlocks it quietly. On the landing she waits and listens, then silently goes downstairs. She checks the kitchen. The door is closed and she can hear classical music playing and her mother preparing the supper. She slips quietly out of the front door.

Scene Fifteen

Characters: Julia, Sam.
It is dark. Julia goes to a local playground which is deserted except for Sam pushing herself on the roundabout.

Sam Jules! I thought you weren't coming. I was just about to go and ring the police and send them round to your house. (*she laughs*) That would be a laugh, wouldn't it? I'd love to see your old man's face then. Hope you've got my little parcel with you?

Julia It's not yours.

Sam It is now. Finders keepers, eh?

Julia You didn't find it. You stole it.

Sam Yeah, and dead easy it was, too. Told some stupid nurse I was a community visitor for your old lady. Asked where her room was. She told me, the stupid fool. Didn't bat an eyelid. It was simple after that. I just had to wait a week or two for my chance. Let's have it then.

Julia No, I'm going to give it back to Mrs Altman.

Sam (*mocking her*) What, you're going to fight me for it, are you?

Julia It's not yours.

Sam Listen, you stupid little git, if you take that back now they'll definitely think it was you.

Julia I'll tell them it was you.

Sam Oh, yeah? Who's going to believe you? Hasn't got my fingerprints on it – but I bet it's got yours. So give.

Julia starts to back off but Sam grabs her.

Sam Don't be daft. You don't want to get hurt.

She rips the button off Julia's jacket, takes the bracelet, and shoves Julia to the ground.

Sam Thanks for looking after it so nicely for me. They did raid my old man's. Found all that stuff he nicked from Parkside Court last week. I knew they would. He's so stupid. He should have got rid of it, like I did. See you then. Oh, and don't forget I want that money by tomorrow.

Sam swaggers off whistling. Julia gets up slowly, angry and humiliated. She screams and kicks the roundabout and then sits on it, her head down. She is crying.

Scene Sixteen

Characters: Mrs Altman, Julia.

Later that evening. Mrs Altman is sitting in her room reading. There is a frantic knocking on her door.

Mrs Altman   Do come in. There's no need to batter the door down.

Julia rushes in, clearly upset.

Mrs Altman   My dear, it's you! Whatever is it?

Julia is crying too much to speak so Mrs Altman puts her arm round her and they sit on the bed.

Mrs Altman   Now, what on earth's the matter?

She reaches for a tissue and hands it to Julia and waits patiently for her to calm down.

Mrs Altman   There, that's better. Do you feel like talking now? (*Julia nods*) Fire away then, dear girl, I'm all ears.

Julia   It's . . . it's about . . .

Mrs Altman   My bracelet?

Julia   Yes. I know, I know where . . . oh!

Mrs Altman   You know where it is?

Julia   Yes, but I didn't take it. I didn't!

Mrs Altman   Now, calm down, my dear. Don't go getting all upset again. I've told you, haven't I, a dozen times that I don't believe you'd steal from me so just tell me all about it and I'll call Miss Barnes and we'll get the whole thing sorted out. Don't worry, I won't let them get the police again.

Julia   I don't care if they do. I've had enough. I'm going to tell the truth and I don't care who believes me!

Mrs Altman   Good for you. That's the spirit. Is this about that ghastly girl who seems to meet up with you whenever you leave this place?

Julia	What? You know about Sam?
Mrs Altman	Oh, I haven't got the slightest idea who she is but I've seen her from my window a few times and I don't like the look of her, I can tell you. Is she being all right to you, dear? (*Julia doesn't answer*) You can trust me, you know. Come on. Tell me about it. (*smiling*) I shan't bite.
Julia	She's just horrible to me.
Mrs Altman	Bullying you, you mean? (*Julia nods miserably*) I thought as much. And you haven't told your parents? The school? Well, she has got you frightened, hasn't she? But all is not lost, I will –
Julia	(*interrupting her*) But I took money! From Mum.
Mrs Altman	For this girl?
Julia	Yes.
Mrs Altman	Threatening you? (*Julia nods*) Well, there you are then. Hardly for yourself, was it? Oh, admittedly it was wrong but I know your mother and father. When they know what's been going on they'll understand.
Julia	Mum won't.
Mrs Altman	No, I'm sure she will. Clash a bit, do you? Mm, with me it was my father. Nothing I did ever seemed right for him but I realised later that he loved me very much. He simply wanted me to do my best and not throw my opportunities away. Your mother's probably the same.
Julia	That's what Dad says. He says we're too like each other. That's why we don't get on.
Mrs Altman	It'll change, you'll see, when you're older. Now, to get back to this miserable girl. I've seen her hanging about here a couple of times and I asked the staff whether she was a visitor like you, but nobody seemed to know her. Then when Mabel, one of our cleaners, told me this girl had asked about me, I

certainly had my suspicions but unfortunately there wasn't much I could do about it as nobody seems to have seen her on the day the bracelet was taken. But if you speak up, then together I think we might just have a chance of catching her out. What do you think, my dear?

Julia   I don't know, but it's your bracelet. Why should she have it?

Mrs Altman   Why indeed? So tell me what's happened and I'm sure we can get this all sorted out. Feeling better?

Julia   Yes.

Mrs Altman   Good. Telling someone's always the most difficult thing but if they're a good friend they won't let you down. These people mustn't be allowed to get away with it. So, tell me everything and then we'll get Miss Barnes.

The End

SPEAKING AND LISTENING ACTIVITIES

Help Notes can be found on pages 177–180.

FOOTBALL CRAZY

INDIVIDUAL (Help Notes 1)

1 **My favourite sport.** Prepare a talk on your favourite sport, either one you participate in or one that you like watching.

Points you might consider:
- how you became involved
- your experiences of playing/watching
- trophies won
- favourite professionals.

2 **Sport isn't everything.** Prepare a talk on why you don't like sport and your other interests instead.

Points you might consider:
- why you think sport's not important
- something else you prefer to do
- why this is better.

PAIRS OR GROUPS (Help Notes 2)

3 **Everybody should have to do sports at school.** Discuss this giving opinions for and against.

Points you might consider:
- health
- enjoyment
- team spirit
- talent
- winning
- aggression
- fans misbehaving

- shouldn't be compulsory
- boring
- can't/don't want to
- other talents are just as important.

4 Girls should be allowed to take part in any sport they want and schools should provide the facilities for them. Discuss this giving opinions for and against.

Points you might consider:
- separate changing facilities
- staffing
- timetable
- enough pupils interested
- physical strength
- talent
- funding.

5 Running away doesn't solve anything. Discuss this giving as many views as possible.

Points you might consider:
- facing problems
- talking about it to someone
- causes upset
- only way to handle it
- draws attention to problem
- puts you in danger.

6 There's too much sport on television. Discuss this giving opinions for and against.

Points you might consider:
- how much on each week
- which sports shown most
- not enough less popular sports
- people enjoy/dislike watching sport
- more music and arts programmes needed.

Present the views of the groups to the rest of the class.

WRITING BASED ON ORAL ACTIVITIES

You can choose writing activities from this section that are based on oral work that you have done, or on the oral work of others that you have heard and made notes on. However, you can choose activities for which you have had no oral preparation.

7 Write a *story or playscript* based on sport or running away. The subject could be someone succeeding against all odds, illness or unhappiness, or a struggle against lack of facilities or care. *(Help Notes 3 and 4)*

8 Write a *newspaper report* of a match you have seen. Look in different newspapers to see how sports reports are done as well as reading the Help Notes. *(Help Notes 5)*

9 Design a *leaflet* for new pupils showing all the sports facilities and activities in your school and how to participate. *(Help Notes 6)*

10 Write a *letter* to your local newspaper about the lack of sports facilities in your area. Say what you would like to be done about it but be realistic and reasonable. *(Help Notes 7)*

11 Write a *diary* about a time when you were expected to do really well at something and failed miserably. Write about your experiences – it doesn't have to be sport. What was the occasion? Your feelings? Others' reactions? How did you react and overcome this? *(Help Notes 8)*

HOPING FOR CHARLIE

INDIVIDUAL (Help Notes 1)

1 **Being in hospital.** Prepare a talk about your experiences of being in hospital.

Points you might consider:
- what sort of ward
- how long you were there
- how old you were
- whether it was serious
- how long it took you to recover.

2 **Getting into trouble.** Prepare a talk on your experience of getting into trouble either in or out of school.

Points you might consider:
- when it happened
- how
- what the consequences were
- who was to blame
- whether you were punished.

PAIRS OR GROUPS (Help Notes 2)

3 **Appearances.** Discuss why appearance and being good-looking seem so important and then prepare a talk.

Points you might consider:
- judging on appearance rather than personality or behaviour
- role of the media, TV, magazines, adverts, films
- combating discrimination and prejudice.

4 **Differences between schools.** Discuss the differences between your school and Charlie's school, and prepare a talk. *(See Notes on Hoping for Charlie, pages 66–67.)*

Points you might consider:
- better/worse things
- rules
- uniform
- teachers

- homework
- timetable
- freedom
- friends.

5 The disabled. Prepare a talk about the disabled.

Points you might consider:
- talk about anyone you know who is disabled, either physically or mentally
- how families cope
- whether ordinary schools should cater for those who are disabled
- what the community can do
- name calling
- why this happens
- how it can be stopped and people encouraged to have more respect for the disabled.

6 There must be life on other planets. Prepare a talk on this.

Points you might consider:
- there must be so many galaxies
- UFOs seen here
- aliens have visited earth
- we can't be the only intelligent species
- space travel a reality.

Present the views of the groups to the rest of the class.

WRITING BASED ON ORAL ACTIVITIES

You can choose writing activities from this section that are based on oral work that you have done, or on the oral work of others that you have heard and made notes on. However, you can choose activities for which you have had no oral preparation.

7 Write a *story or playscript* about aliens, or a hospital. *(Help Notes 3 and 4)*

8 Write a *newspaper report* about a group of residents who are opposed to a home for the mentally handicapped being set up by a Health Care Trust in their road. Give all the details and report on interviews with both sides. *(Help Notes 5)*

9 Write a *letter* to your local newspaper either objecting to this home in your road or welcoming it, giving full reasons for your views. *(Help Notes 7)*

10 Design a *leaflet* which a local health authority wants you to produce for a hospital or health clinic giving information about its wards, staff, what it specialises in, its A & E unit and so on. *(Help Notes 6)*

11 You are a patient, or nurse, or doctor. Write a *diary* that is set in a hospital. *(Help Notes 8)*

THE RUSSIAN BRACELET

INDIVIDUAL (Help Notes 1)

1 Being bullied/Being a bully. Prepare a talk on your experiences of being bullied or being a bully.

Points you might consider:
- why this happened
- whether you could have avoided it
- what you did
- whether teachers or parents were involved
- how you coped
- whether it's different now
- why this might be the case.

2 Being old. Prepare a talk on old age.

Points you might consider:
- physical changes
- difficulties
- prejudice
- help needed
- medical care
- loss of independence
- more leisure time
- being a grandparent.

PAIRS OR GROUPS (Help Notes 2)

3 Honesty. Prepare a talk about whether it is worth being honest.

Points you might consider:
- whether we can always be honest
- whether it's kinder to lie sometimes
- when to believe people
- whether it's possible to be totally trustworthy.

4 Friendship and trust. Should Julia have told Mrs Altman or her parents earlier about Sam and the bullying?

Points you might consider:
- whether it would have made things worse/better
- how she could prove it
- whether Mrs Altman was right to trust Julia
- whether Julia's mum was too hard on her.

5 Violence. Discuss what causes people to use threats and violence against others.

Points you might consider:
- whether violence is an answer to problems
- other methods that can be used to get rid of anger and hatred
- the role of TV and films
- whether there is a time when violence is justified
- whether girls are becoming more violent
- why this might be so, and what can be done about it.

6 Old people deserve respect. Prepare a talk on this.

Points you might consider:
- have a lot of experience of life
- need looking after
- often on their own
- can help us with lots of things
- are entertaining
- their memories are interesting
- can tell us about the past
- we shouldn't take advantage of frail people.

Present the views of the groups to the rest of the class.

WRITING BASED ON ORAL ACTIVITIES

You can choose writing activities from this section that are based on oral work that you have done, or on the oral work of others that you have heard and made notes on. However, you can choose activities for which you have had no oral preparation.

7 Write a *story or playscript* about someone who is asked to tell the truth but doesn't want to because it would be too hurtful, or put someone in danger. What are the consequences of this? *(Help Notes 3 and 4)*

8 Write a *newspaper report* based on being the victim of bullying. Do some research, ask questions of both pupils, parents and teachers. *(Help Notes 5)*

9 Write a *letter* to a local newspaper about old people in your area asking for volunteer help. Describe how rewarding it is to befriend the elderly. *(Help Notes 7)*

10 Design a *leaflet* for crime prevention for older people, or bullying for your age group. Include what to look out for, how you can avoid being a victim, who to contact, support groups. *(Help Notes 6)*

11 Write a *diary* about being bullied, or living in an old people's home. Do some research first about your chosen subject. *(Help Notes 8)*

HELP NOTES

1 INDIVIDUAL ORAL WORK

- Your talk should not be less than three minutes long, so practise it aloud and time it.
- Have headings and key words to remind you of what to say.
- Don't read it or learn it off by heart.
- Speak to the whole class, not just the teacher, and try to stand still.
- Use visual aids, such as photos, if possible.
- Have a good vocabulary and avoid slang.
- Use all of your allowed time.
- Speak clearly and loudly enough for everyone to hear.

2 PAIRS AND GROUP ORAL WORK

- Prepare well by noting down your group's thoughts and views.
- Make it clear and interesting with good vocabulary.
- Encourage those who are not saying much to join in.
- When you present your talk let everybody have something to say.
- Be aware of your audience, and speak directly and clearly to them.

3 STORY WRITING

- Plan your story. What is the plot? Who are the main characters?
- Have an exciting beginning to hold the readers' interest.
- Develop the story giving as much detail as possible but don't stray away from your main story-line, and keep up the suspense or interest.
- Use paragraphs, correct punctuation and spelling, and speech marks where needed.

- Check what you've written. Re-write if you have to.
- Have a strong ending that shows the story is finished.

4 PLAY SCRIPTS

- Look at the lay-out of the plays in this book. Separate the dialogue (what is said) from the characters' names with a clear space, and do not use speech marks.
- Have a story-line for your play and think carefully about the characters. Don't make them all the same.
- Compile a list of characters as you write.
- Use scenes but don't make them too short.
- Introduce each scene with a list of characters, and say where the scene takes place and what the characters are doing when they begin the scene.
- Separate your directions (what you want the actors to do) from the dialogue, but short directions such as (*pause*) should be in brackets and italics if possible.
- Think of the drama and make it exciting and interesting.

5 NEWSPAPER REPORT/ARTICLE

- Do some research to gather both facts and opinions. Talk to people and look at newspapers, magazines and other sources in the library.
- A report is not an essay so use columns, sub-headings, graphs and lists, and speech marks to quote exactly what was said.
- Use these five as a guide: *what* happened, *who* is involved, *when*, *where*, and *how* did it happen?
- Give full details but don't write a novel. Be short and sharp.
- Remember the human interest and interview.

6 DESIGNING A LEAFLET

- Decide what type of leaflet: information, campaign, publicity?
- Fold your paper into two or three sections so it's easier to read.

- Who is it for? Have an eye-catching title page, short headings and plenty of space.
- Don't use large chunks of text (writing) as it won't be read. Give essential information *briefly*.
- Use graphics (drawings, illustrations) in colour if possible.
- Include all relevant information, contact names, addresses and telephone numbers and say who produced the leaflet – for example, CAFCA Campaign For Cleaner Air.

7 A LETTER

- Letters may be formal, for example to a newspaper editor or to a company. Or they may be informal, for example to a friend or relative. Informal letters can be written any way you want but formal letters must be set out in a specific way.

(YOUR ADDRESS)   32 Farm Lane
                                Lower Hanbury
                                Wiltshire
                                SP1 3YY

(DATE)   day/month/year

The Editor   *(NAME)*
Wiltshire Courier   *(ADDRESS YOU ARE WRITING TO)*
Market Street
Salisbury
Wiltshire SP1 4MS

Dear Editor,

I was interested in your article on . . .

Yours sincerely,

(Your signature)

Charmian King *(your name printed)*

8 A DIARY

- Diaries are very personal records of your thoughts and experiences. They are usually written every day.
- Diaries are always written in the first person – for example, *I did this; I was glad about that.*
- You can use notes or full sentences and set out your diary exactly as you like, using illustrations if you want.

.